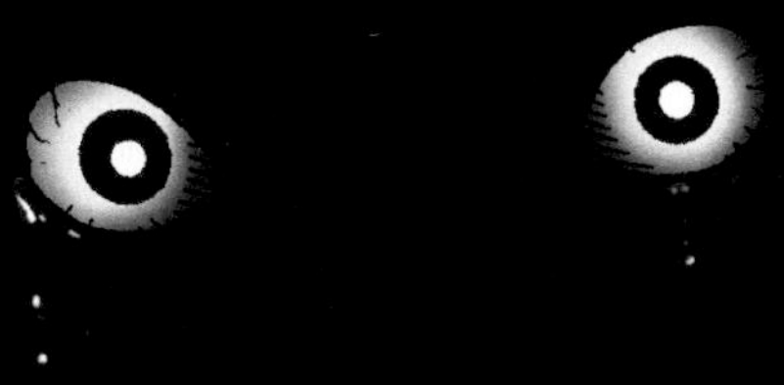

BATMAN THE KILLING JOKE

THE DELUXE EDITION

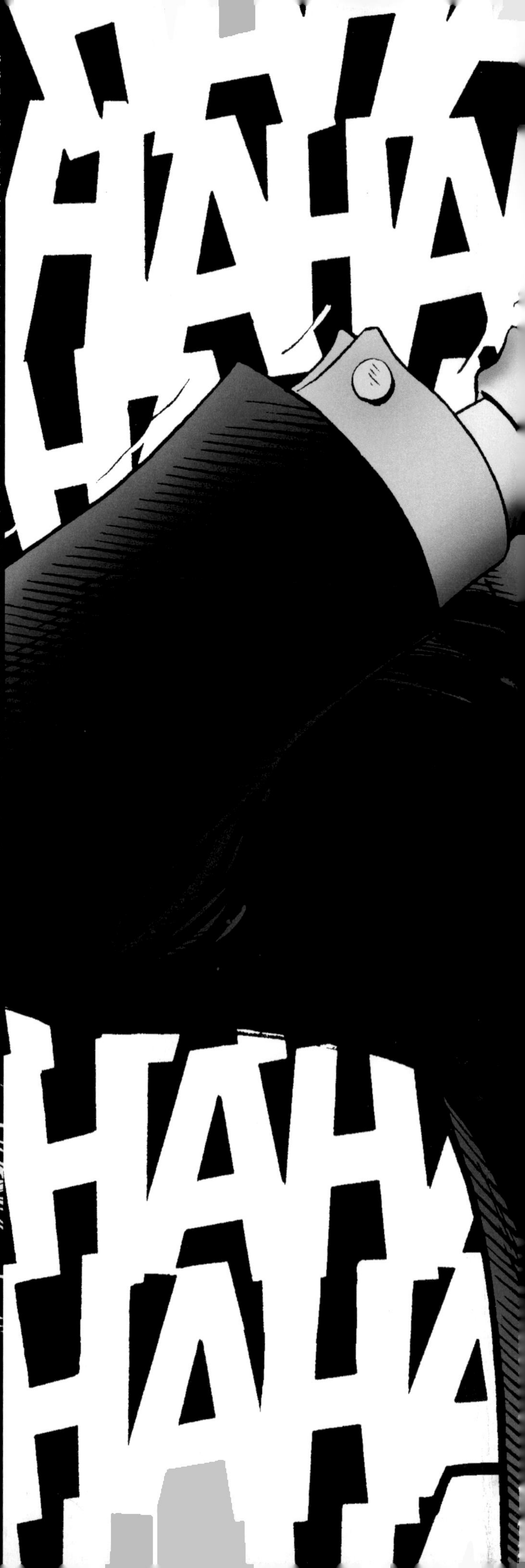
HAHA
HAHA

Denny O'Neil, Mark Chiarello Editors – Original Series
Robbin Brosterman Design Director – Books
Louis Prandi Publication Design

Bob Harras Senior VP – Editor-in-Chief, DC Comics

Diane Nelson President
Dan DiDio and **Jim Lee** Co-Publishers
Geoff Johns Chief Creative Officer
John Rood Executive VP – Sales, Marketing & Business Development
Amy Genkins Senior VP – Business & Legal Affairs
Nairi Gardiner Senior VP – Finance
Jeff Boison VP – Publishing Planning
Mark Chiarello VP – Art Direction & Design
John Cunningham VP – Marketing
Terri Cunningham VP – Editorial Administration
Alison Gill Senior VP – Manufacturing & Operations
Hank Kanalz Senior VP – Vertigo & Integrated Publishing
Jay Kogan VP – Business & Legal Affairs, Publishing
Jack Mahan VP – Business Affairs, Talent
Nick Napolitano VP – Manufacturing Administration
Sue Pohja VP – Book Sales
Courtney Simmons Senior VP – Publicity
Bob Wayne Senior VP – Sales

Cover by **Brian Bolland**

Batman: The Killing Joke: The Deluxe Edition

DC Comics, 1700 Broadway, New York, NY 10019
A Warner Bros. Entertainment Company
Printed in the USA. Twelfth Printing.
ISBN 978-1-4012-1667-2

Library of Congress Cataloging-in-Publication Data

Moore, Alan, 1953-
Batman : the killing joke : the deluxe edition / Alan Moore, Brian Bolland. -- Deluxe ed.
p. cm.
"Originally published in BATMAN: THE KILLING JOKE, BATMAN BLACK AND WHITE 4."
ISBN 978-1-4012-1667-2
1. Graphic novels. I. Bolland, Brian. II. Title.
PN6728.B36M663 2012
741.5'973–dc23
2012017683

SUSTAINABLE FORESTRY INITIATIVE
Certified Chain of Custody
At Least 20% Certified Forest Content
www.sfiprogram.org
SFI-01042
APPLIES TO TEXT STOCK ONLY

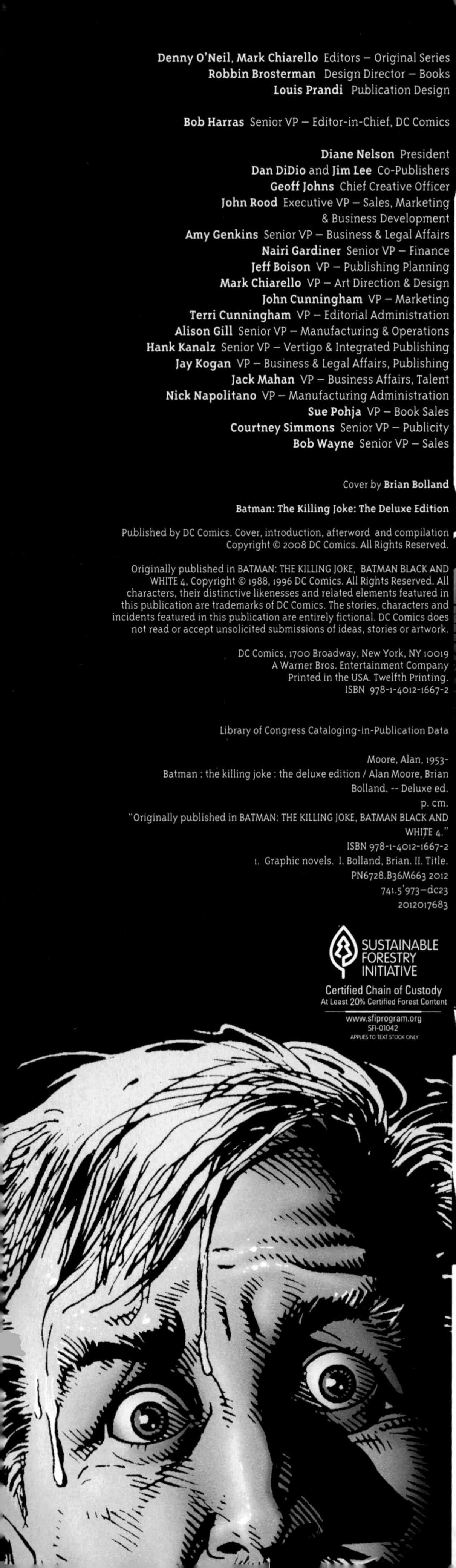

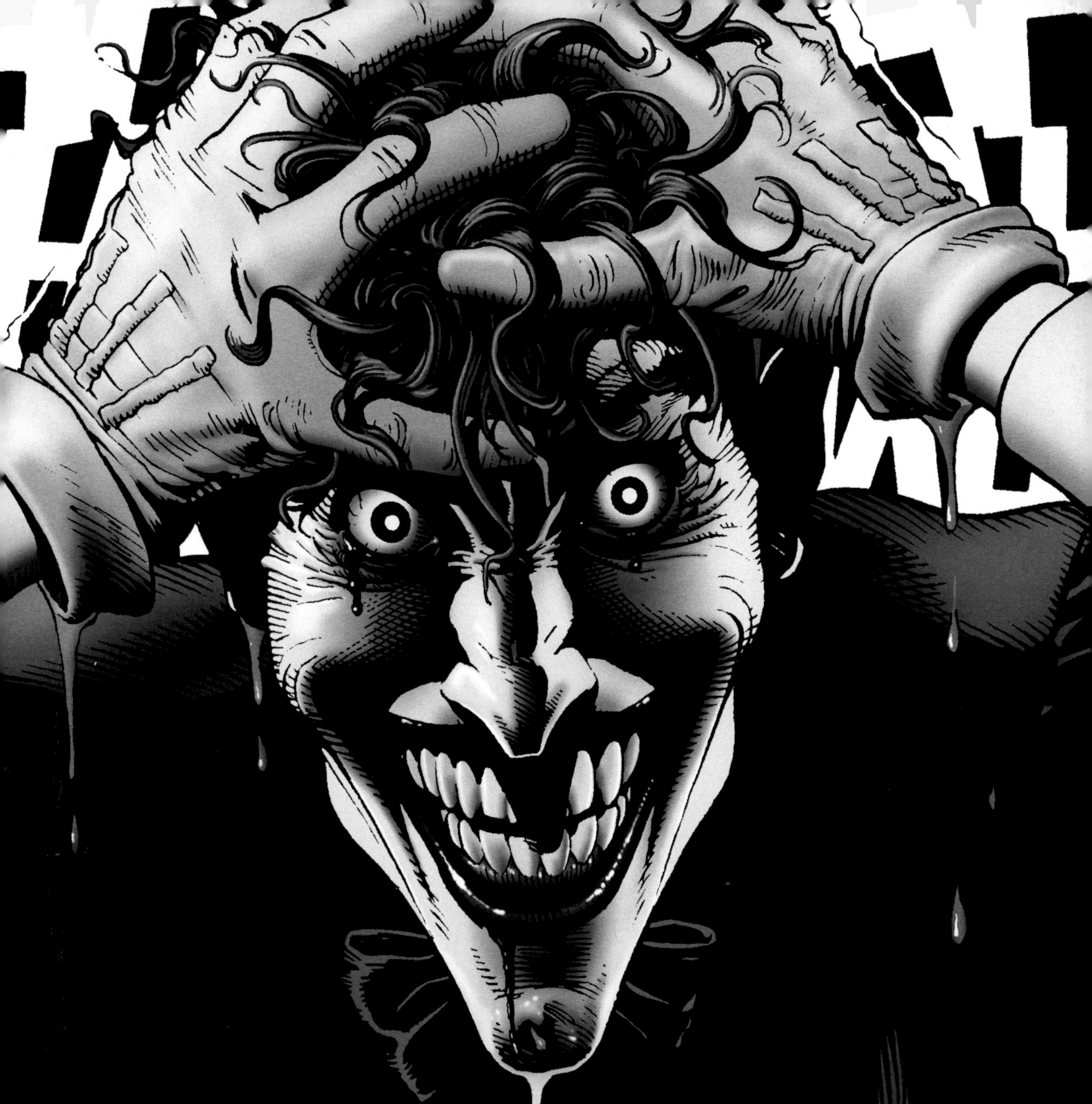

BATMAN THE KILLING JOKE

THE DELUXE EDITION

Alan Moore Writer   Brian Bolland Art and Colors   Richard Starkings Letterer

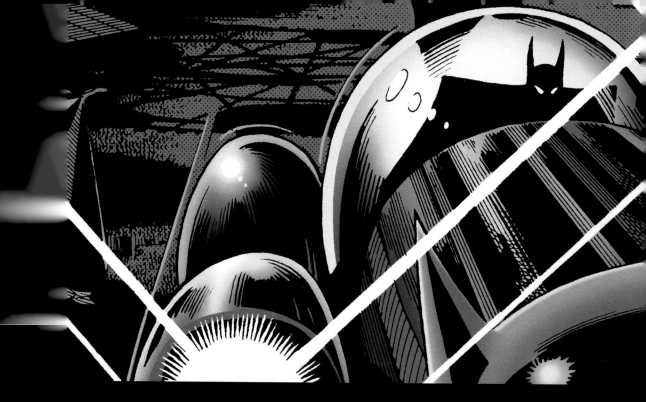

INTRODUCTION

Man, how cool is this?

Like everyone who was in the mainstream comics field in the late 1980s, or — as was my case — had their noses pressed against the glass, the back-to-back-to-back-to-back of DARK KNIGHT RETURNS, WATCHMEN, BATMAN: YEAR ONE, and BATMAN: THE KILLING JOKE, completely reenergized the field. The characters (other than those in WATCHMEN) had been around for decades and, while many talented writers and artists had done much notable work in that time, there was an incredible sense of the new coming from Frank Miller and this handful of crazy Brits — Alan Moore, Brian Bolland, John Higgins, Richard Starkings and Dave Gibbons — who were seeing possibilities in them, in the kinds of stories that could be told, and not incidentally, in the way that a story could be presented.

BATMAN: THE KILLING JOKE is the only one of the stories listed above that did not first exist in another format, as a series of comics that were eventually collected into that catch-all term, a "graphic novel." THE KILLING JOKE was a 46-page story, but it was crafted at such an astonishing level, and printed so much more cleanly and carefully, that it seemed to be a different beast altogether, not just a really great Batman comic, but something different. I didn't get it then, but I do now.

That is what authors of extraordinary craft can do:

And thrilling. Don't forget thrilling.

I am told that the origins of BATMAN: THE KILLING JOKE go back to a Batman/Judge Dredd proposal that Moore and Bolland had cooked up. When it fell through, Moore asked Bolland what else he wanted to do, and Bolland said, "The Joker, please."

So polite. And thus a classic was born.

Moore is famous for many things, not the least of which are his maniacally controlled and precisely orchestrated scripts, requiring an equal and similar effort from his artist partner, and in the amazing Brian Bolland he found an artist his equal in talent, fanaticism, care, and expressiveness. Both excel in impressing with their rendering of the mundane, so that it never *feels* mundane. And then they blast into a reveal, a money shot so explosive that is it only then that you realize how well you, as a reader, have been lulled to rest *on purpose*, just to set you up.

The Joker's reveal on page 11, the tragic event on page 18, the second reveal on page 37, all orchestrated and carried out in ways that astonish, and then astonish again when you go back and see just how much these artists have known and set things up from the beginning. How fun it is to be in the hands of creators who know so much about what they are doing.

Priceless, funny, and perfect for the characters of Batman and The Joker.

What you hold in your hands, though, is not the book that I own, that so inflamed(!) me and thousands of others back in 1988, because of one crucial element: the coloring.

This time around, you lucky buggers, you have the fantastic treat to see the book colored by the artist himself, and see his more complete vision of how the story should look. Side by side, the comparison is amazing.

Bolland's colors are characteristically thoughtful and restrained. They fit the work more completely than Higgins's state-of-the-art job in 1988 and are a joy to look at. Slow down and one can see how cool the palette is now, versus the warmer one of 1988, and how much better that reflects the somber tone of the story, and how, when Bolland retains a color from 1988 that has become iconic, like Barbara's yellow shirt, he integrates that so well into the cooler colors in the scene, allowing the shirt to really pop and ratchet up the horror of the event.

But the biggest and most amazing change in this newly colored edition is in the flashback sequences.

Bolland washes out all color in each one, but chooses to spotlight an object in each — a bowl of tentacles, shrimp, and so on — in increasingly

intense shades of red, all leading up to (here's that sense that everything has been planned from the start by masterful hands) the Red Hood that was posited to be The Joker's mostly forgotten origin, *way back in 1951*, and the transformation of the milquetoast failed comedian to insane criminal mastermind.

Brrrrrr. I just got chills.

Anyone else get chills?

Man, how cool is this?

Tim Sale

Pasadena, CA 2008

Tim Sale lives in southern California with his aged dogs Hotspur and Shelby. Raised in Seattle, he still finds California an odd place, though he hopes that will change someday.

Tim is the artist on BATMAN: DARK VICTORY, CATWOMAN: WHEN IN ROME, BATMAN: THE LONG HALLOWEEN and many other titles.

In 2006, Tim became the artist for the hit NBC television series Heroes.

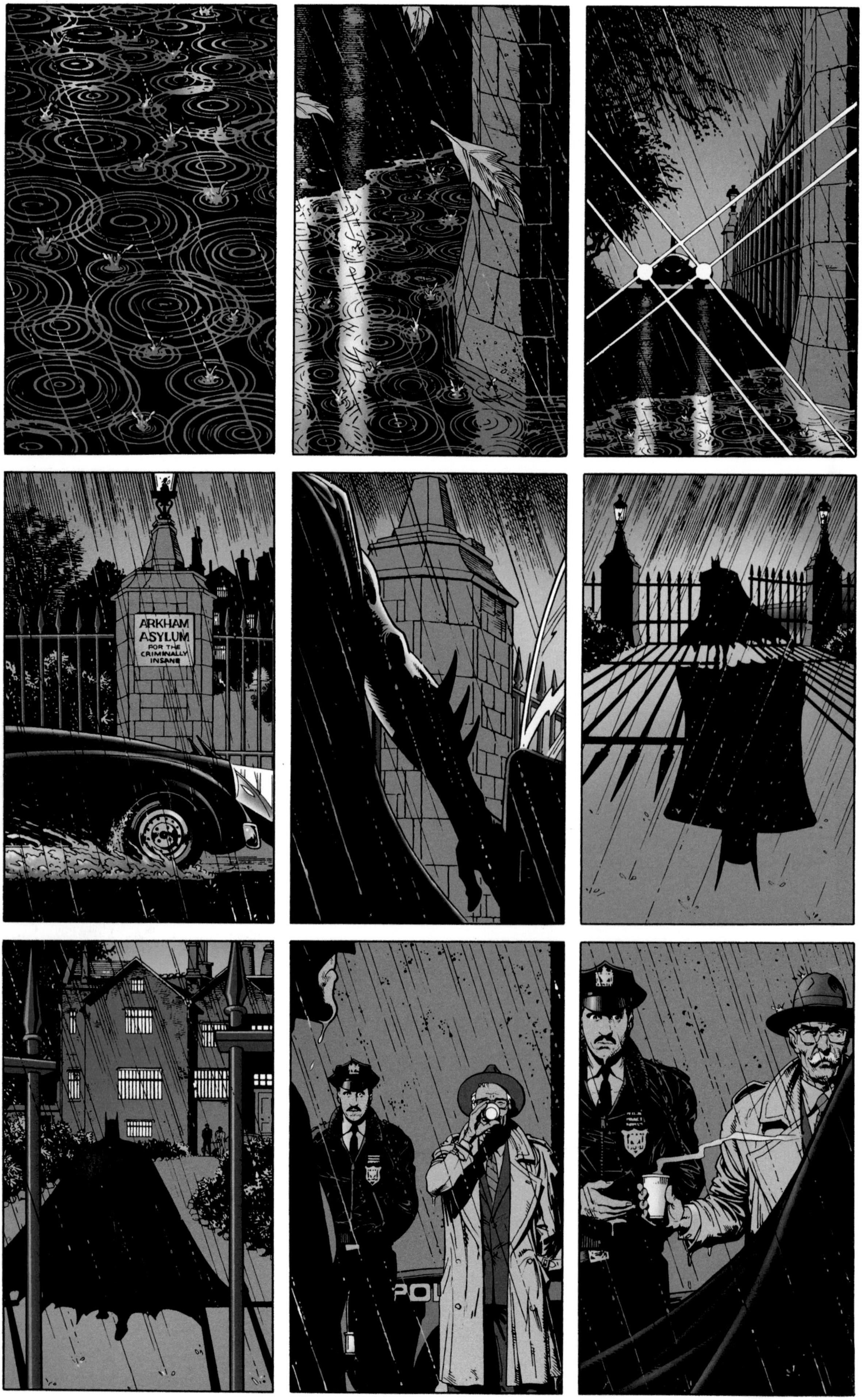
ARKHAM ASYLUM FOR THE CRIMINALLY INSANE
POL

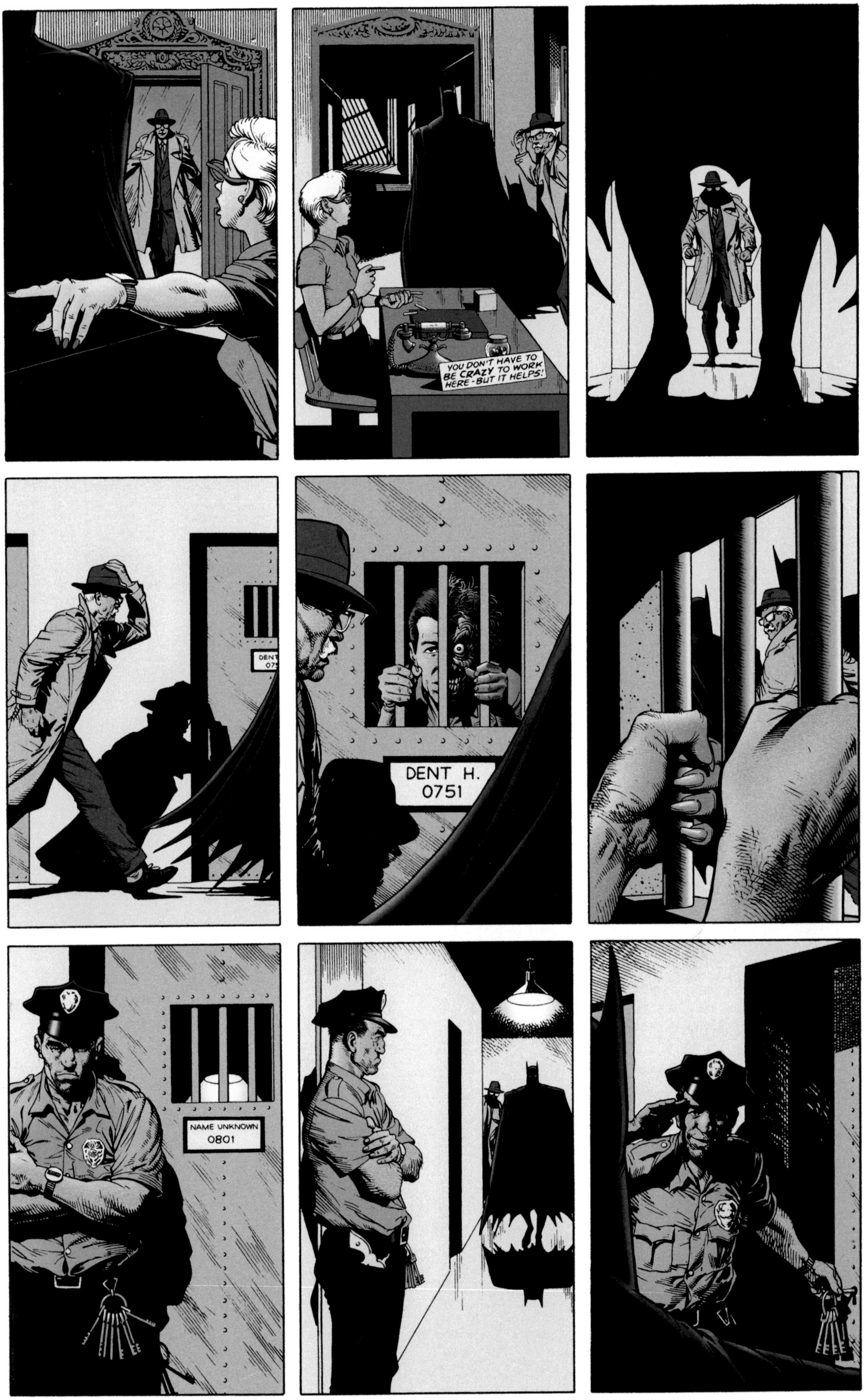
YOU DON'T HAVE TO BE CRAZY TO WORK HERE-BUT IT HELPS!
DENT H. 0751
NAME UNKNOWN 0801

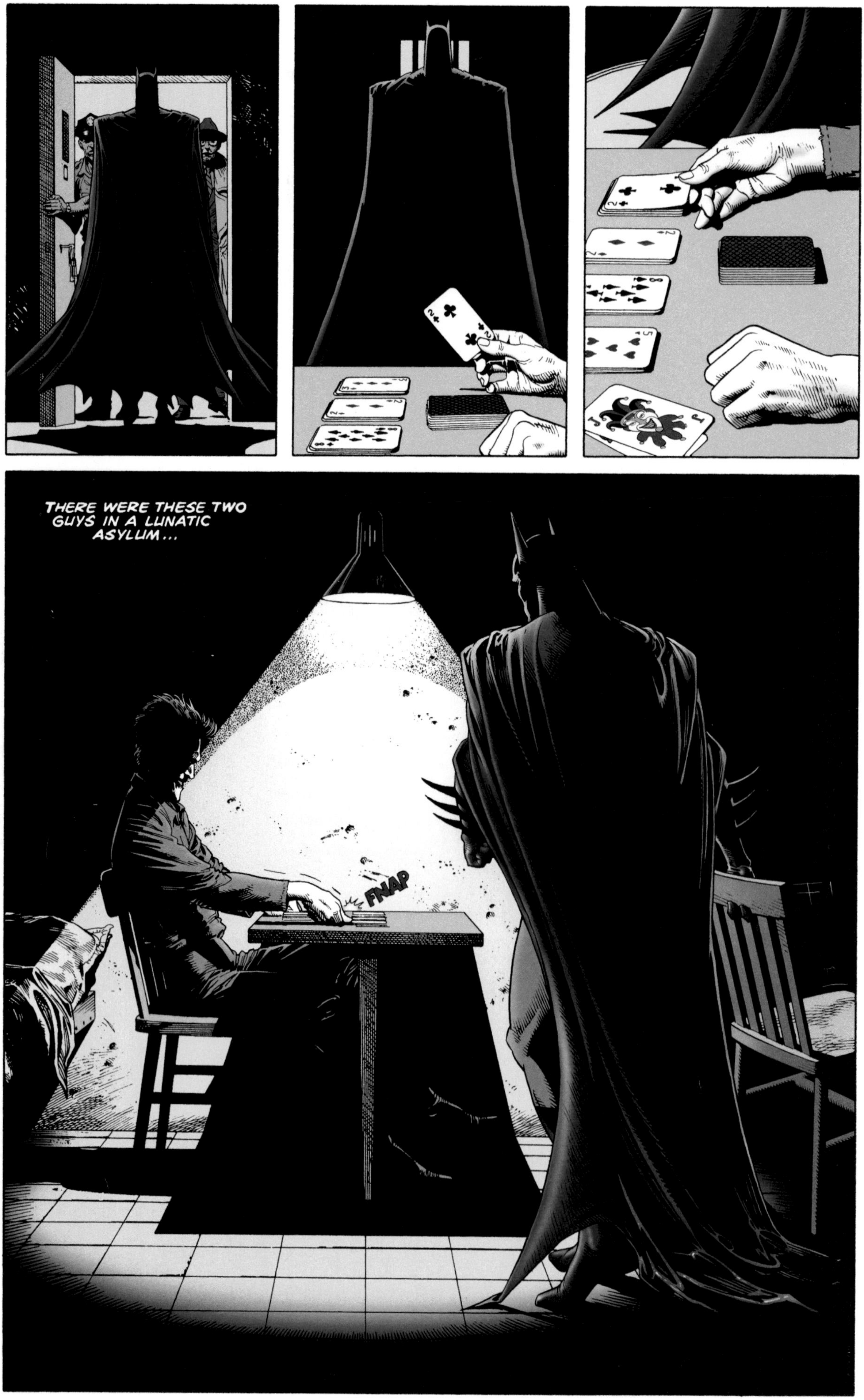
THERE WERE THESE TWO GUYS IN A LUNATIC ASYLUM...
FNAP

HELLO.

I CAME TO TALK.

I'VE BEEN *THINKING* LATELY. ABOUT YOU AND ME.

ABOUT WHAT'S GOING TO *HAPPEN* TO US, IN THE *END.*

WE'RE GOING TO *KILL* EACH OTHER, AREN'T WE?

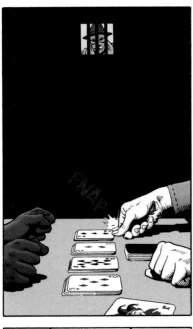

PERHAPS YOU'LL KILL ME, PERHAPS I'LL KILL YOU, PERHAPS SOONER, PERHAPS LATER.

I JUST WANTED TO KNOW THAT I'D MADE A *GENUINE* ATTEMPT TO TALK THINGS *OVER* AND *AVERT* THAT OUTCOME.

JUST *ONCE.*

ARE YOU *LISTENING* TO ME? IT'S *LIFE AND DEATH* THAT I'M DISCUSSING HERE.

MAYBE *MY* DEATH...

...MAYBE *YOURS.*

I DON'T FULLY UNDERSTAND WHY OURS SHOULD BE SUCH A *FATAL* RELATIONSHIP, BUT I DON'T WANT YOUR *MURDER* ON MY...

...HANDS...

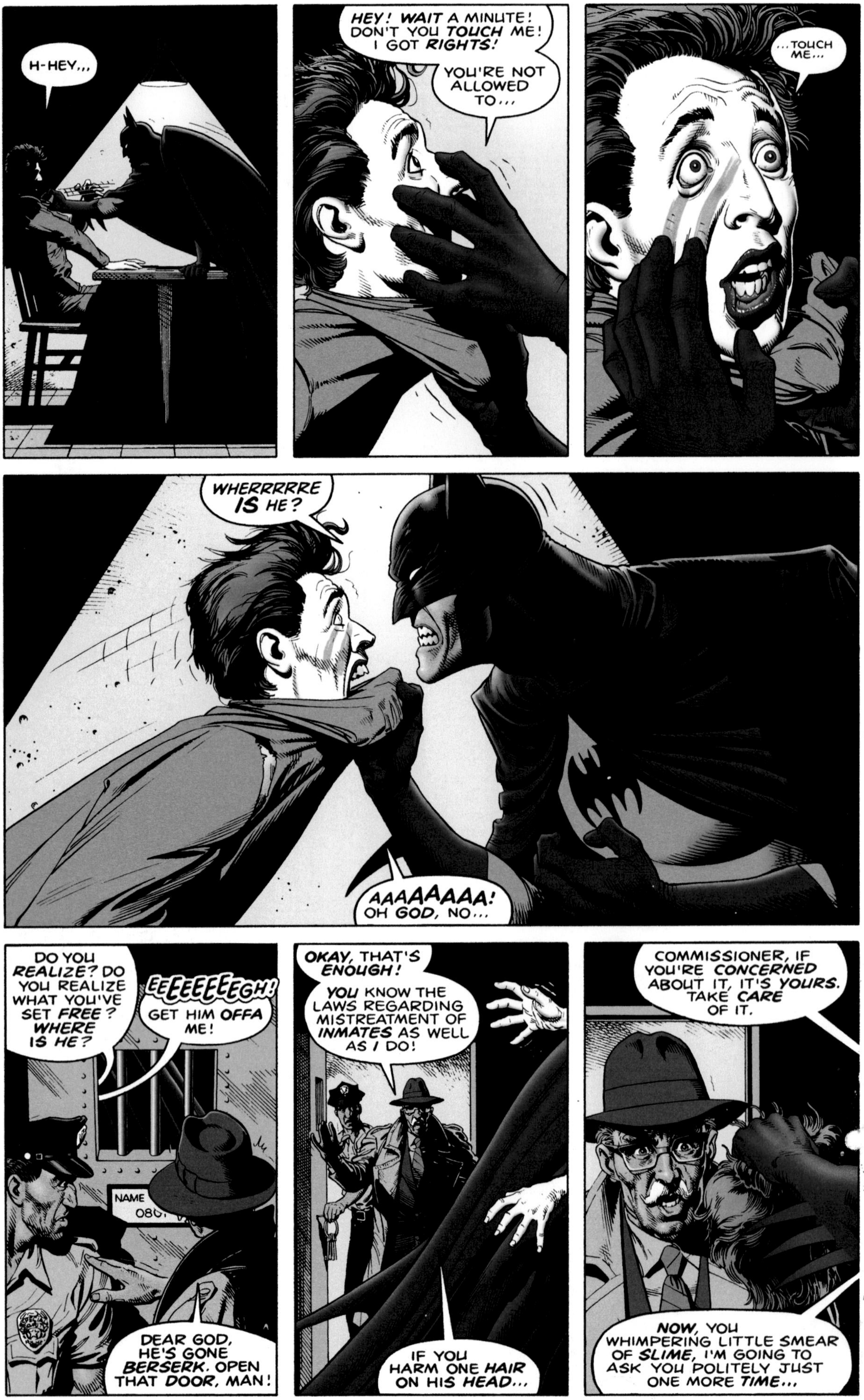
H-HEY,,,
HEY! WAIT A MINUTE! DON'T YOU TOUCH ME! I GOT RIGHTS!
YOU'RE NOT ALLOWED TO...
...TOUCH ME...
WHERRRRRE IS HE?
AAAAAAAA! OH GOD, NO...
DO YOU REALIZE? DO YOU REALIZE WHAT YOU'VE SET FREE? WHERE IS HE?
EEEEEEEEGH! GET HIM OFFA ME!
NAME
DEAR GOD, HE'S GONE BERSERK. OPEN THAT DOOR, MAN!
OKAY, THAT'S ENOUGH!
YOU KNOW THE LAWS REGARDING MISTREATMENT OF INMATES AS WELL AS I DO!
IF YOU HARM ONE HAIR ON HIS HEAD...
COMMISSIONER, IF YOU'RE CONCERNED ABOUT IT, IT'S YOURS. TAKE CARE OF IT.
NOW, YOU WHIMPERING LITTLE SMEAR OF SLIME, I'M GOING TO ASK YOU POLITELY JUST ONE MORE TIME...

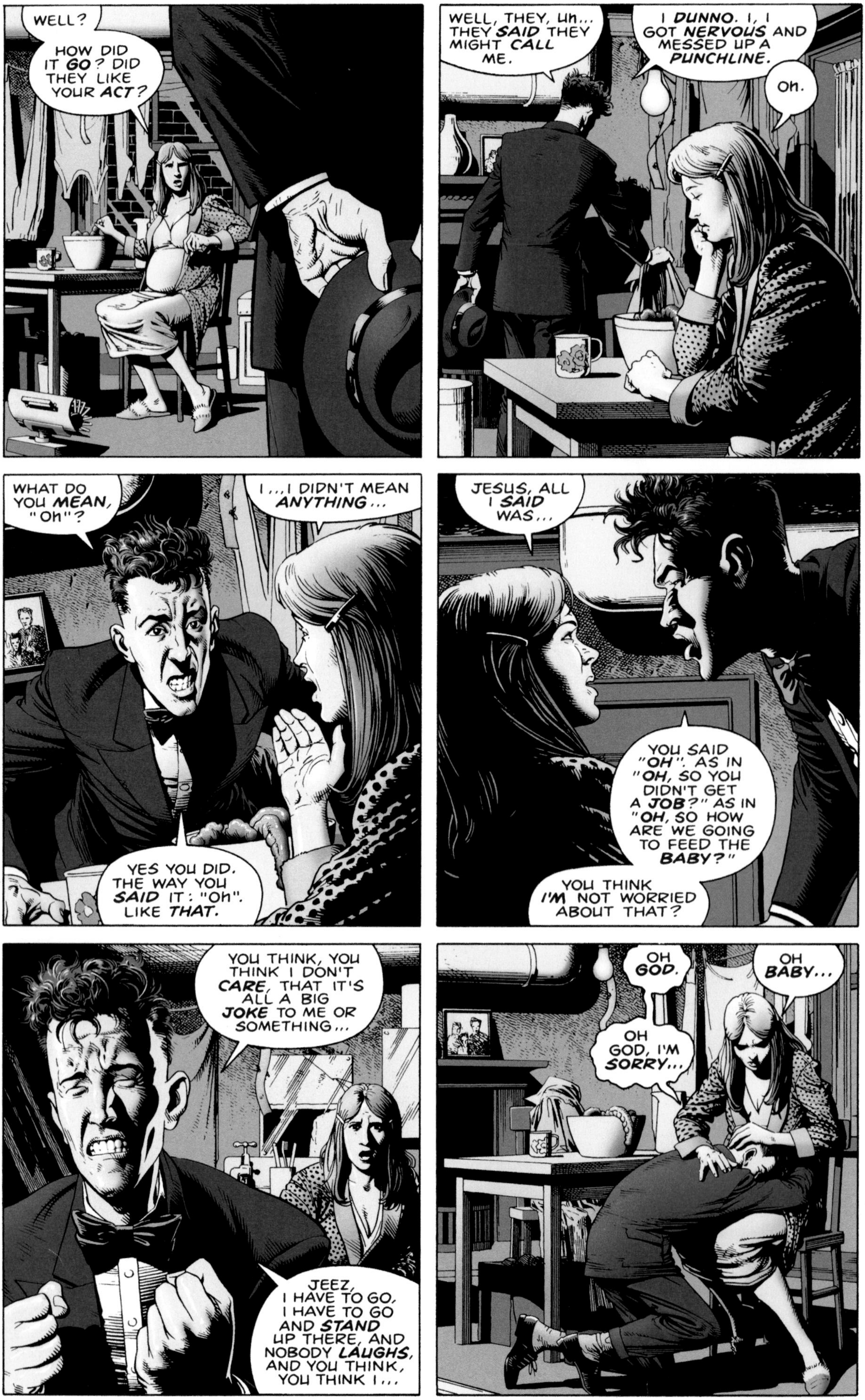
WELL?
HOW DID IT GO? DID THEY LIKE YOUR ACT?
WELL, THEY, uh... THEY SAID THEY MIGHT CALL ME.
I DUNNO. I, I GOT NERVOUS AND MESSED UP A PUNCHLINE.
Oh.
WHAT DO YOU MEAN, "Oh"?
I... I DIDN'T MEAN ANYTHING...
YES YOU DID. THE WAY YOU SAID IT: "Oh". LIKE THAT.
JESUS, ALL I SAID WAS...
YOU SAID "OH". AS IN "OH, SO YOU DIDN'T GET A JOB?" AS IN "OH, SO HOW ARE WE GOING TO FEED THE BABY?"
YOU THINK I'M NOT WORRIED ABOUT THAT?
YOU THINK, YOU THINK I DON'T CARE, THAT IT'S ALL A BIG JOKE TO ME OR SOMETHING...
JEEZ, I HAVE TO GO, I HAVE TO GO AND STAND UP THERE, AND NOBODY LAUGHS, AND YOU THINK, YOU THINK I...
OH GOD.
OH BABY...
OH GOD, I'M SORRY...

I DON'T MEAN TO TAKE IT OUT ON *YOU*. YOU'RE SUH-SUFFERING *ENOUGH*, BEING MARRIED TO A *LOSER*.

HONEY, THAT'S *NOT*...

IT'S *TRUE*. I CAN'T *SUPPORT* YOU. OH JEANNIE, WHAT ARE WE GOING TO *DO*?

IT'LL BE *OKAY*.

JUNIOR WON'T BE HERE FOR ANOTHER *THREE MONTHS*, AND I THINK *MRS. BURKISS* WILL LET THE *RENT* GO A LITTLE LONGER. SHE FEELS *SORRY* FOR ME.

SHE *HATES* ME.

SHE COMES OUT INTO THE *HALLWAY* TO *SCOWL* AT ME EVERY TIME I GO *UPSTAIRS*.

THIS HOUSE STINKS OF *CAT LITTER* AND *OLD PEOPLE*.

I'VE GOT TO GET YOU *OUT* OF HERE BEFORE THE *BABY* COMES...

I JUST WANT ENOUGH *MONEY* TO GET YOU SET UP IN A DECENT *NEIGHBORHOOD*.

THERE ARE GIRLS ON THE *STREET* WHO EARN THAT IN A *WEEKEND* WITHOUT HAVING TO TELL A SINGLE *JOKE*.

HA HA HA HA.

HONEY, DON'T *WORRY*. NOT ABOUT *ANY* OF IT. *I* STILL LOVE YOU, Y'KNOW? JOB OR *NO* JOB, YOU'RE GOOD IN THE *SACK*...

...AND YOU KNOW HOW TO MAKE ME *LAUGH*.

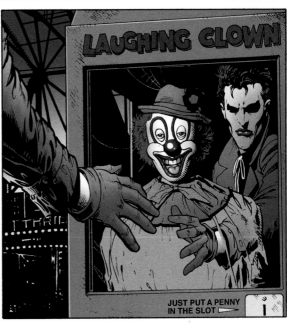

LAUGHING CLOWN

JUST PUT A PENNY IN THE SLOT ➤

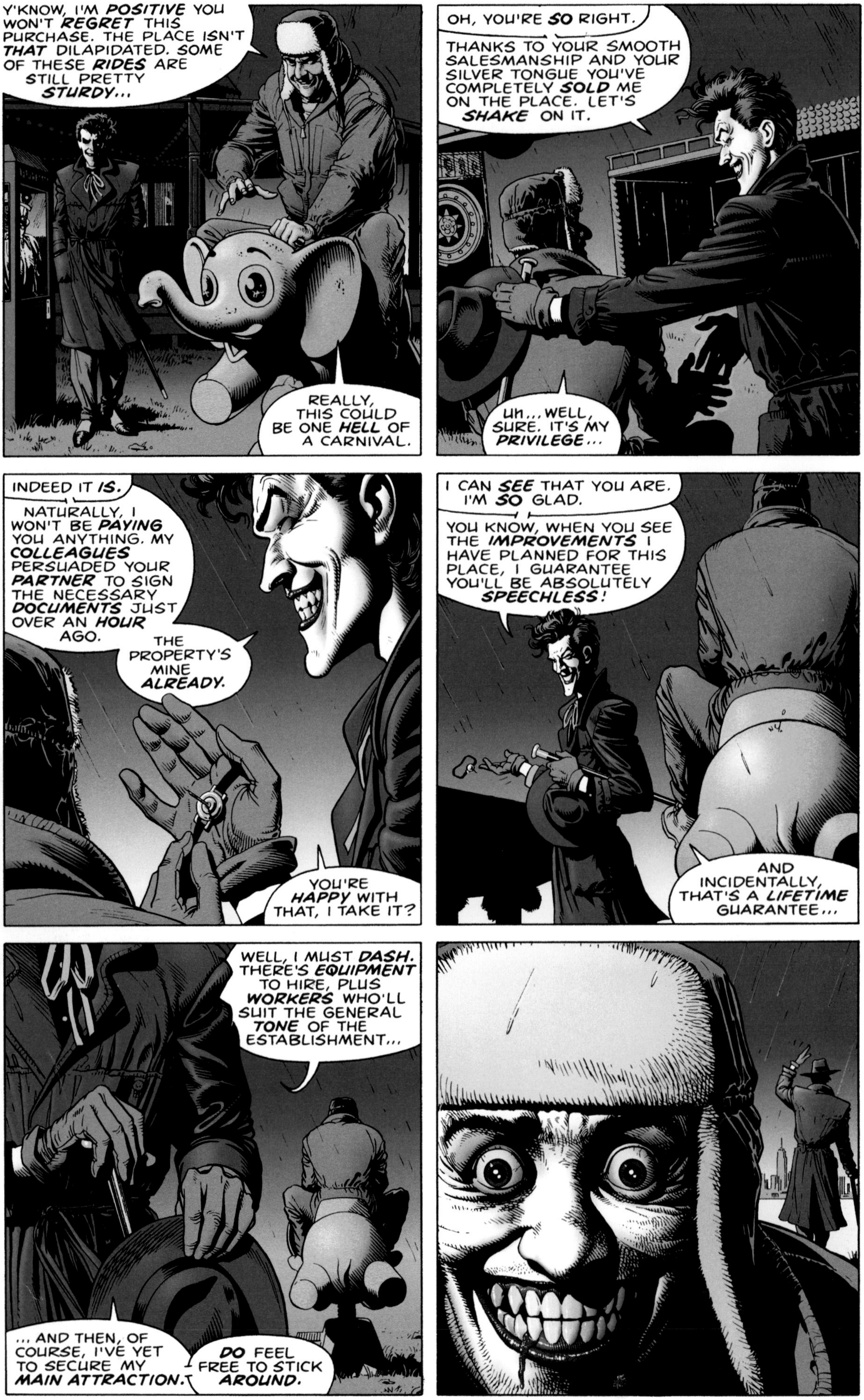
Y'KNOW, I'M POSITIVE YOU WON'T REGRET THIS PURCHASE. THE PLACE ISN'T THAT DILAPIDATED. SOME OF THESE RIDES ARE STILL PRETTY STURDY...
REALLY, THIS COULD BE ONE HELL OF A CARNIVAL.
OH, YOU'RE SO RIGHT.
THANKS TO YOUR SMOOTH SALESMANSHIP AND YOUR SILVER TONGUE YOU'VE COMPLETELY SOLD ME ON THE PLACE. LET'S SHAKE ON IT.
UH... WELL, SURE. IT'S MY PRIVILEGE...
INDEED IT IS.
NATURALLY, I WON'T BE PAYING YOU ANYTHING. MY COLLEAGUES PERSUADED YOUR PARTNER TO SIGN THE NECESSARY DOCUMENTS JUST OVER AN HOUR AGO.
THE PROPERTY'S MINE ALREADY.
YOU'RE HAPPY WITH THAT, I TAKE IT?
I CAN SEE THAT YOU ARE. I'M SO GLAD.
YOU KNOW, WHEN YOU SEE THE IMPROVEMENTS I HAVE PLANNED FOR THIS PLACE, I GUARANTEE YOU'LL BE ABSOLUTELY SPEECHLESS!
AND INCIDENTALLY, THAT'S A LIFETIME GUARANTEE...
WELL, I MUST DASH. THERE'S EQUIPMENT TO HIRE, PLUS WORKERS WHO'LL SUIT THE GENERAL TONE OF THE ESTABLISHMENT...
... AND THEN, OF COURSE, I'VE YET TO SECURE MY MAIN ATTRACTION.
DO FEEL FREE TO STICK AROUND.

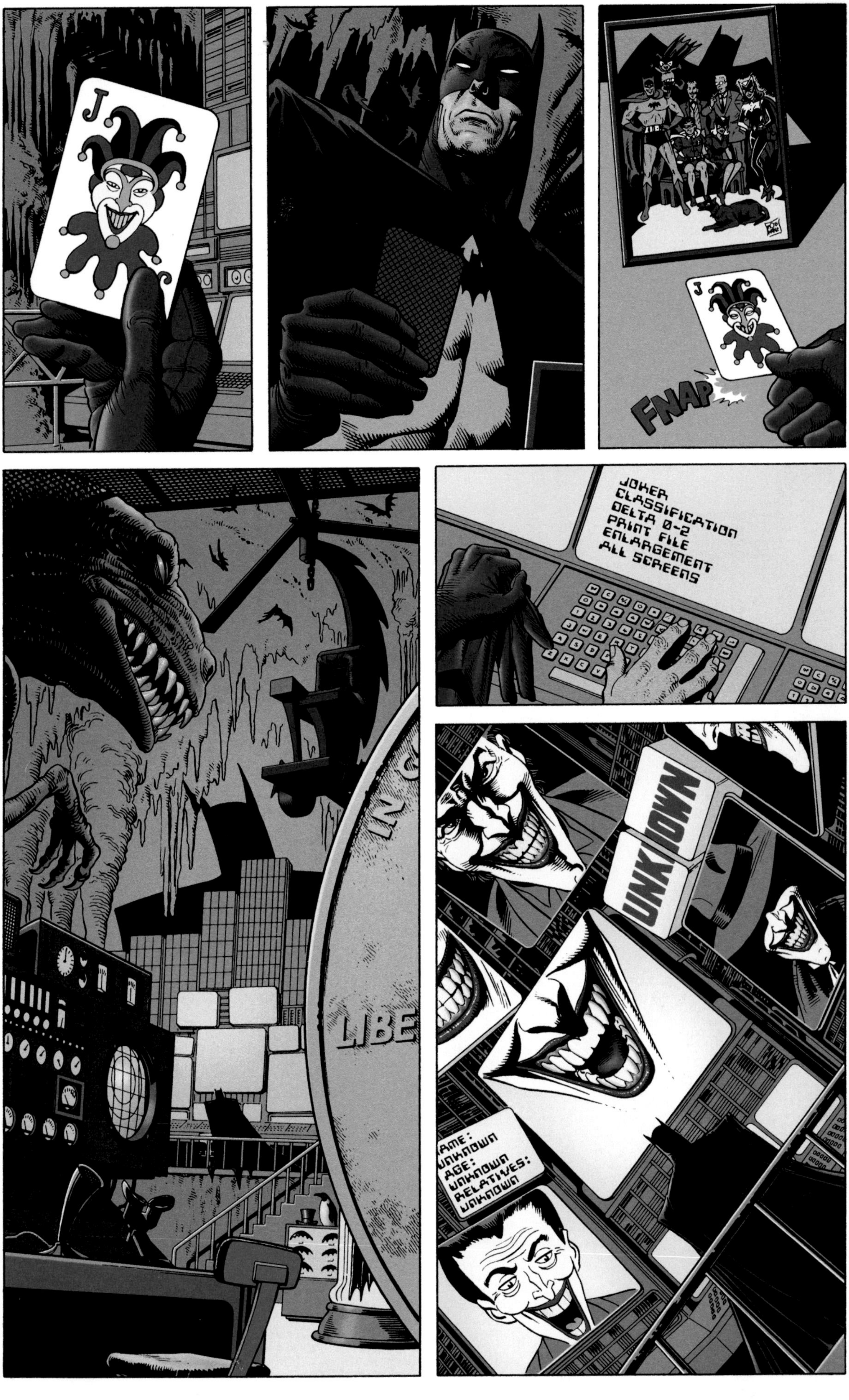
FNAP
JOKER
CLASSIFICATION
DELTA 0-2
PRINT FILE
ENLARGEMENT
ALL SCREENS
UNKNOWN
AME:
UNKNOWN
AGE:
UNKNOWN
RELATIVES:
UNKNOWN

YOUR **REFRESHMENTS**, SIR.

MASTER BRUCE?

IS THERE ANYTHING **FURTHER** I CAN ASSIST WITH, OR WILL THAT BE **ALL**?

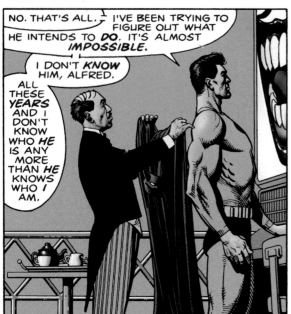

NO. THAT'S **ALL.** I'VE BEEN TRYING TO FIGURE OUT WHAT HE INTENDS TO **DO.** IT'S ALMOST **IMPOSSIBLE.**

I DON'T **KNOW** HIM, ALFRED.

ALL THESE **YEARS** AND I DON'T KNOW WHO **HE** IS ANY MORE THAN **HE** KNOWS WHO **I** AM.

HOW CAN TWO PEOPLE **HATE** SO MUCH WITHOUT **KNOWING** EACH OTHER?

I *HATE* THIS. WHENEVER WE *JAIL* HIM, I THINK "PLEASE GOD, *KEEP* HIM THERE." THEN HE *ESCAPES* AND WE ALL SIT ROUND HOPING HE WON'T DO ANYTHING *TOO* AWFUL THIS TIME.

OTHAM EXAMINER
ASYLUM SECURITY UPROAR
MANIAC ESCAPES AGAIN

CRIMEFIGHTER UNAVAILABLE FOR CO
VICKI VALE EXCLUSIVE

I *HATE* IT.

DAD, JUST *ONCE* COULD YOU LEAVE YOUR WORK AT THE *OFFICE* AND *RELAX*? I MADE YOU *COCOA*.

THANK YOU, SWEETHEART. I'LL DRINK IT WHEN I'VE PASTED THIS LATEST *CLIPPING* IN.

ALBUM

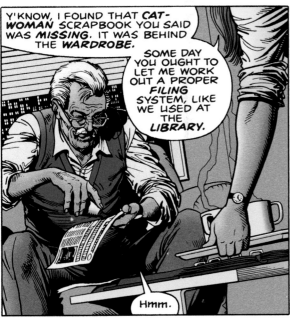

Y'KNOW, I FOUND THAT *CAT-WOMAN* SCRAPBOOK YOU SAID WAS *MISSING*. IT WAS BEHIND THE *WARDROBE*.

SOME DAY YOU OUGHT TO LET ME WORK OUT A PROPER *FILING* SYSTEM, LIKE WE USED AT THE *LIBRARY*.

Hmm.

URRGH. LOOK, YOU USED TOO MUCH *PASTE*! IT'S ALL SQUIDGING UNDER THE EDGES OF THE *CLIPPING*. YOU'RE GOING TO GET IT ON YOUR *PANTS*...

BARBARA, YOU'RE *FUSSIER* THAN YOUR *MOTHER* WA...

WAS THAT THE *DOOR*?

YEAH. IT'LL BE *COLLEEN* FROM ACROSS THE STREET. TONIGHT'S OUR *YOGA* CLASS.

C'MON, DAD... *COMPANY*! PUT YOUR *SCRAPBOOKS* AWAY.

BAT-GARBED VIGILANTE CRITICALLY INJURES MURDERER

DISFIGURED HOMICIDAL MANIAC IN HOSPITAL

HEH. LOOK AT *THIS* ONE. FIRST TIME THEY *MET*. NOW WHAT *YEAR* WAS THAT?

WELL, I REMEMBER YOU DESCRIBING THE *WHITE FACE* AND THE *GREEN HAIR* TO ME WHEN I WAS A KID. SCARED THE *HELL* OUT OF ME.

I THOUGHT YOU'D BE *INTERESTED*...

YEAH, WELL, I HAD SOME INTERESTING *NIGHTMARES*.

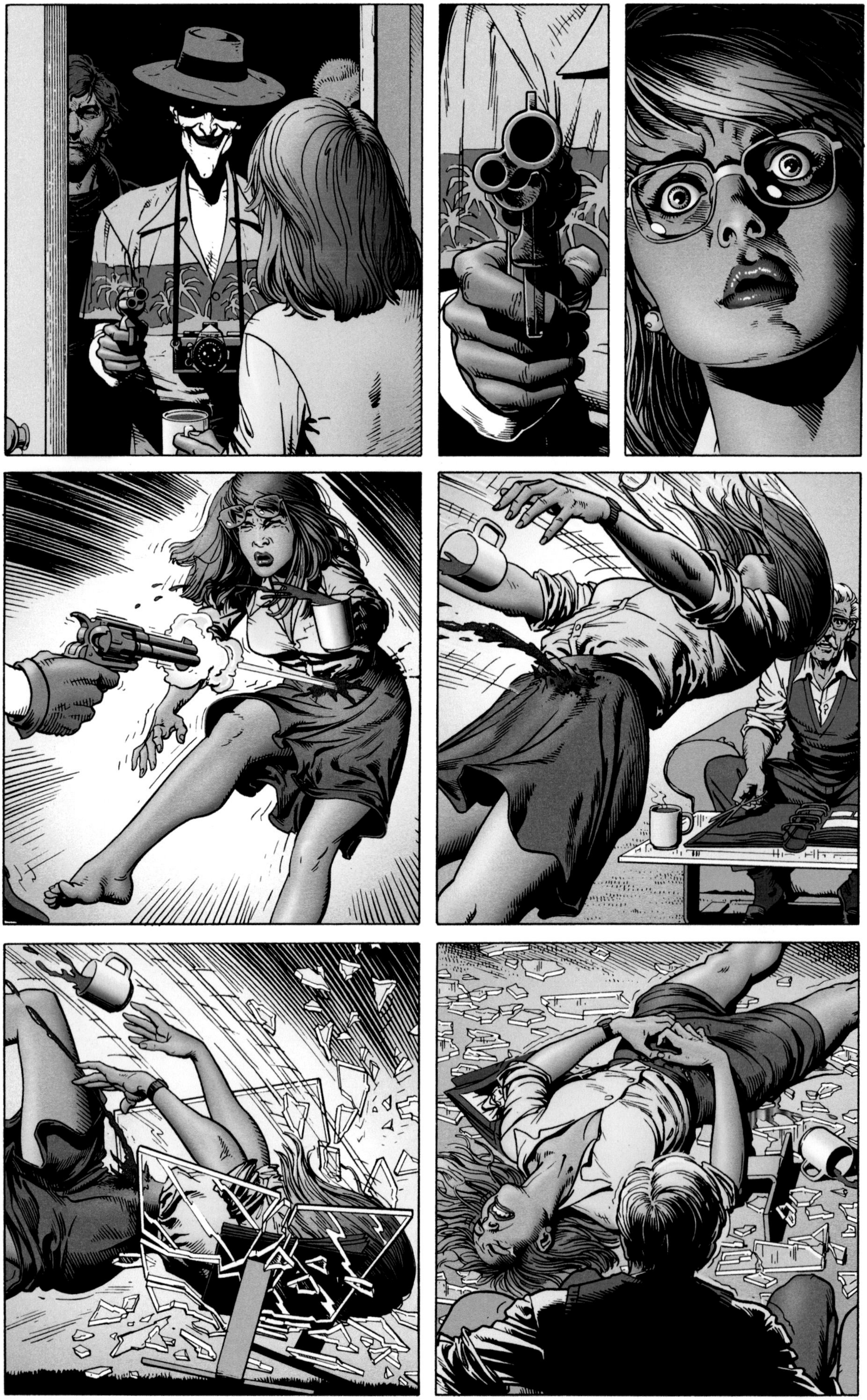

BARB..?

PLEASE DON'T *WORRY.* IT'S A PSYCHOLOGICAL COMPLAINT, COMMON AMONGST EX-LIBRARIANS. YOU SEE, SHE THINKS SHE'S A *COFFEE TABLE* EDITION...

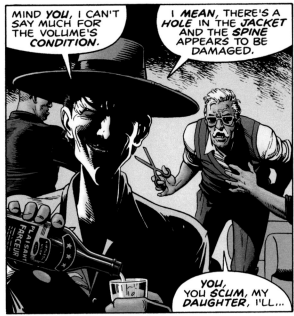

MIND *YOU,* I CAN'T SAY MUCH FOR THE VOLUME'S *CONDITION.*

I *MEAN,* THERE'S A *HOLE* IN THE *JACKET* AND THE *SPINE* APPEARS TO BE *DAMAGED.*

YOU, YOU *SCUM,* MY *DAUGHTER,* I'LL...

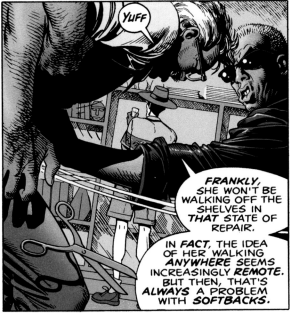

YUFF

FRANKLY, SHE WON'T BE WALKING OFF THE SHELVES IN *THAT* STATE OF REPAIR.

IN *FACT,* THE IDEA OF HER WALKING *ANYWHERE* SEEMS INCREASINGLY *REMOTE.* BUT THEN, THAT'S *ALWAYS* A PROBLEM WITH *SOFTBACKS.*

GOD, THESE *LITERARY DISCUSSIONS* ARE SO *DRY.* WHEN YOU'VE *FINISHED* WITH THE *OLD BOY,* YOU KNOW WHERE TO *TAKE* HIM.

AND *PLEASE...* DO BE *CAREFUL!* AFTER *ALL,* HE IS *TOPPING* THE *BILL.*

YOU KNOW, IT'S *SUCH* A SHAME YOU'LL MISS YOUR FATHER'S *DEBUT,* MISS GORDON.

SADLY, OUR *VENUE* WASN'T *BUILT* WITH THE *DISABLED* IN MIND.

BUT DON'T *WORRY...* I'LL TAKE SOME *SNAPSHOTS* TO *REMIND* HIM OF *YOU.*

WUH... WUH...,WHY... ARE YOU...

DUH... *DOING* THIS..?

TO PROVE A *POINT.*

HERE'S TO *CRIME.*

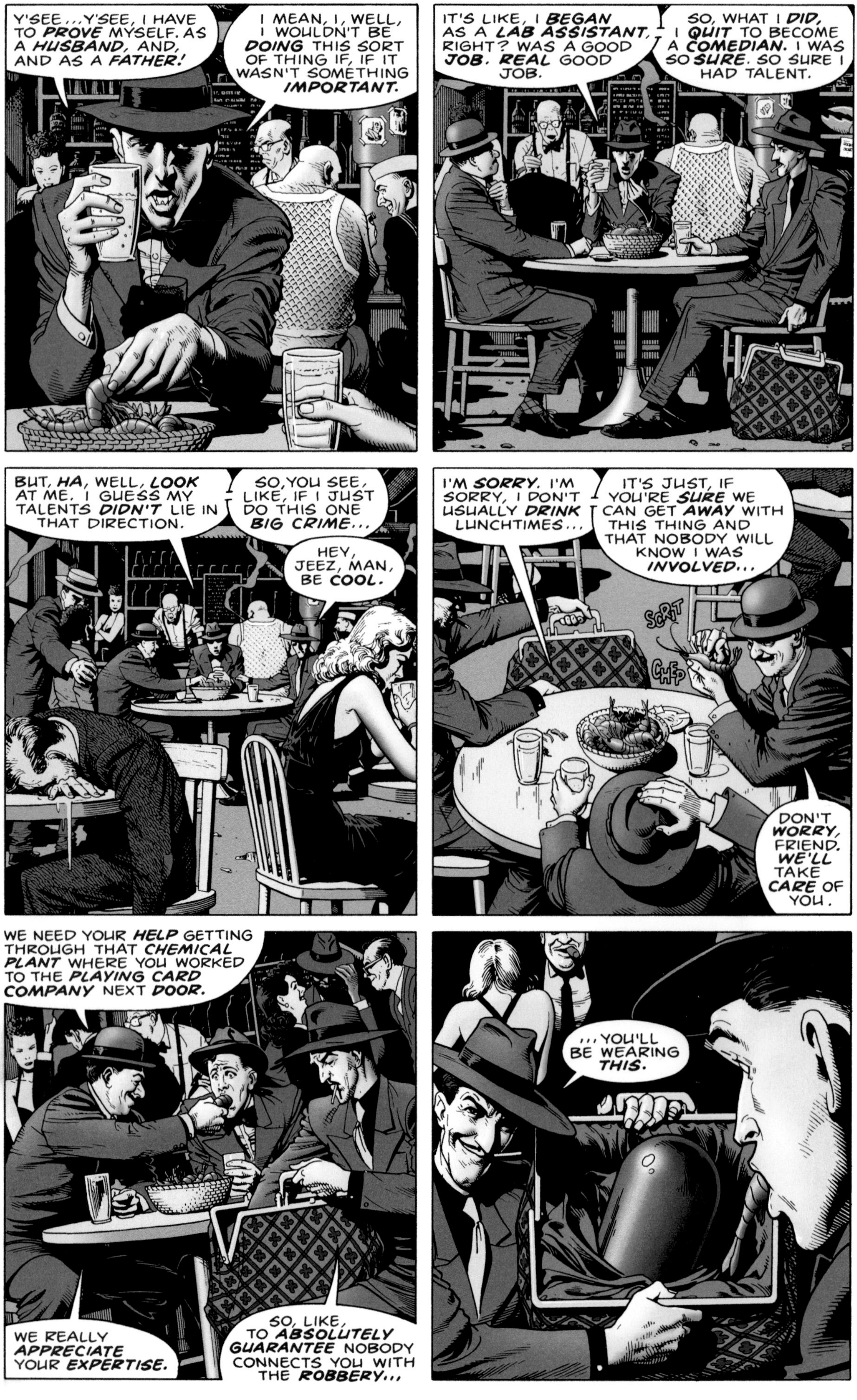

Y'SEE... Y'SEE, I HAVE TO PROVE MYSELF. AS A HUSBAND, AND, AND AS A FATHER!
I MEAN, I, WELL, I WOULDN'T BE DOING THIS SORT OF THING IF, IF IT WASN'T SOMETHING IMPORTANT.
IT'S LIKE, I BEGAN AS A LAB ASSISTANT, RIGHT? WAS A GOOD JOB. REAL GOOD JOB.
SO, WHAT I DID, I QUIT TO BECOME A COMEDIAN. I WAS SO SURE. SO SURE I HAD TALENT.
BUT, HA, WELL, LOOK AT ME. I GUESS MY TALENTS DIDN'T LIE IN THAT DIRECTION.
SO, YOU SEE, LIKE, IF I JUST DO THIS ONE BIG CRIME...
HEY, JEEZ, MAN, BE COOL.
I'M SORRY. I'M SORRY, I DON'T USUALLY DRINK LUNCHTIMES...
IT'S JUST, IF YOU'RE SURE WE CAN GET AWAY WITH THIS THING AND THAT NOBODY WILL KNOW I WAS INVOLVED...
SCRT
CHEP
DON'T WORRY, FRIEND. WE'LL TAKE CARE OF YOU.
WE NEED YOUR HELP GETTING THROUGH THAT CHEMICAL PLANT WHERE YOU WORKED TO THE PLAYING CARD COMPANY NEXT DOOR.
WE REALLY APPRECIATE YOUR EXPERTISE.
SO, LIKE, TO ABSOLUTELY GUARANTEE NOBODY CONNECTS YOU WITH THE ROBBERY...
...YOU'LL BE WEARING THIS.

WEARING..? B-BUT THERE ARE NO *EYE-SLITS*. I WON'T BE ABLE TO *SEE*.

THERE'S THESE LENSES O' RED *TWO-WAY MIRROR GLASS* SET INTO IT. PRETTY SMART *STUFF*, RIGHT?

I, I *DUNNO*. THAT *MASK*... ISN'T IT THE ONE THAT *RED HOOD* GUY WEARS WHO RAIDED THAT *ICE COMPANY* LAST MONTH?

SMARTEN UP. THERE *AIN'T* NO "RED HOOD". THERE'S JUST A BUNCHA *GUYS*, ANNA *MASK*.

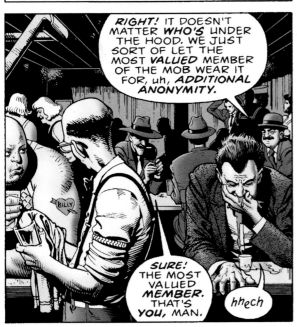

RIGHT! IT DOESN'T MATTER *WHO'S* UNDER THE HOOD. WE JUST SORT OF LET THE MOST *VALUED* MEMBER OF THE MOB WEAR IT FOR, uh, *ADDITIONAL ANONYMITY*.

SURE! THE MOST *VALUED MEMBER*. THAT'S *YOU*, MAN.

hhech

Ahhh, LOOK, REALLY, I DON'T *KNOW*... THAT *CHEMICAL PLANT'S* SO *GRIM* AND *UGLY*. THAT'S PARTLY WHY I *QUIT*.

BUT YOU SAID THERE'S *MINIMAL SECURITY*, MAN.

LISTEN, DO YOU *WANT* TO RAISE YOUR KID IN *POVERTY*?

NO. NO, OF *COURSE* NOT. YOU'RE *RIGHT*. *I MEAN*, IT'S JUST THIS *ONCE*, THEN I CAN SWITCH *NEIGHBORHOODS* AND START A *PROPER* LIFE...

THAT'S THE ATTITUDE! SO... NEXT *FRIDAY NIGHT*, AT *ELEVEN*?

SURE. SURE, WHY *NOT?* HA HA! FRIDAY IT *IS*.

AND THEN, STARTING FROM *SATURDAY MORNING*, I'LL BE *RICH*. I CAN'T *IMAGINE* IT. MY *LIFE'S* GOING TO BE COMPLETELY CHANGED!

NOTHING'S GOING TO BE THE *SAME*...

...NOT EVER *AGAIN*.

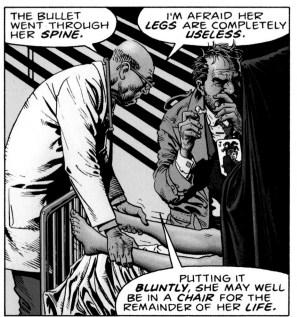

THE BULLET WENT THROUGH HER *SPINE.*

I'M AFRAID HER *LEGS* ARE COMPLETELY *USELESS.*

PUTTING IT *BLUNTLY,* SHE MAY WELL BE IN A *CHAIR* FOR THE REMAINDER OF HER *LIFE.*

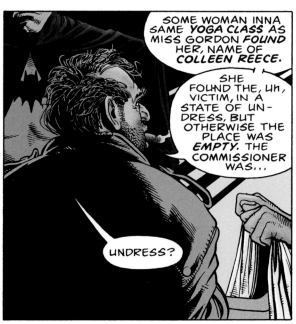

SOME WOMAN INNA SAME *YOGA CLASS* AS MISS GORDON *FOUND* HER, NAME OF *COLLEEN REECE.*

SHE FOUND THE, UH, VICTIM, IN A STATE OF UN-DRESS, BUT OTHERWISE THE PLACE WAS *EMPTY.* THE COMMISSIONER WAS...

UNDRESS?

THEY DIDN'T *TELL* YOU? HE'D REMOVED HER *CLOTHING* AFTER *SHOOTING* HER. WE, uh... WELL, WE FOUND A *LENS-CAP* ON THE FLOOR THAT DIDN'T FIT ANY CAMERA IN THE PLACE. WE BELIEVE THAT, uhh...

WELL, THAT HE TOOK SOME *PICTURES.*

OF HER.

JEEZ, LOOK, REALLY, I'M *SORRY.* I THOUGHT YOU *KNEW.* IT'S PRETTY *SICK,* AIN'T IT?

YES.

PRETTY SICK.

PLEASE LEAVE US ALONE FOR A MOMENT.

CLIC

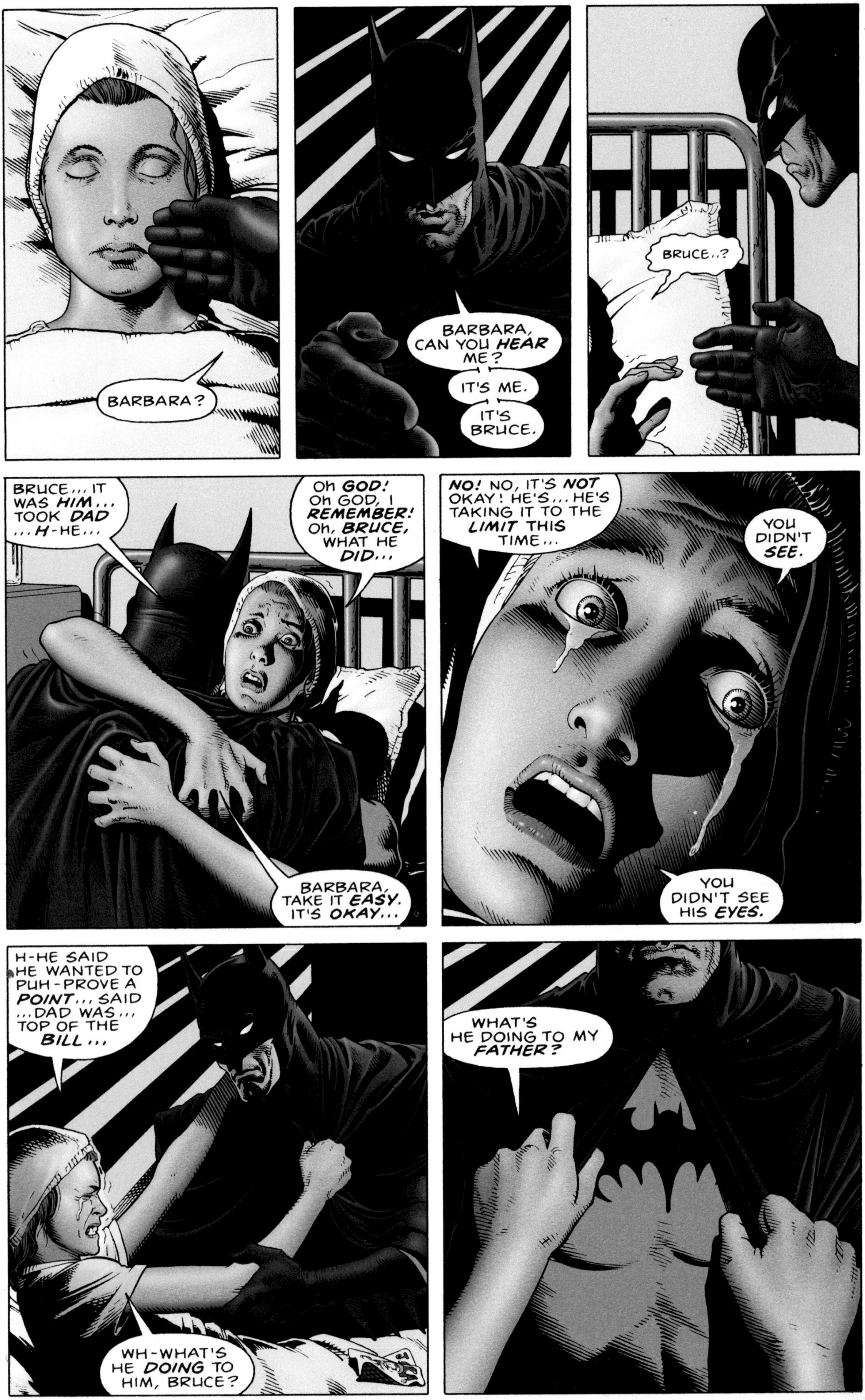
BARBARA?
BARBARA, CAN YOU HEAR ME?
IT'S ME.
IT'S BRUCE.
BRUCE..?
BRUCE... IT WAS HIM... TOOK DAD ...H-HE...
Oh GOD! Oh GOD, I REMEMBER! Oh, BRUCE, WHAT HE DID...
BARBARA, TAKE IT EASY. IT'S OKAY...
NO! NO, IT'S NOT OKAY! HE'S... HE'S TAKING IT TO THE LIMIT THIS TIME...
YOU DIDN'T SEE.
YOU DIDN'T SEE HIS EYES.
H-HE SAID HE WANTED TO PUH-PROVE A POINT... SAID ...DAD WAS... TOP OF THE BILL...
WH-WHAT'S HE DOING TO HIM, BRUCE?
WHAT'S HE DOING TO MY FATHER?

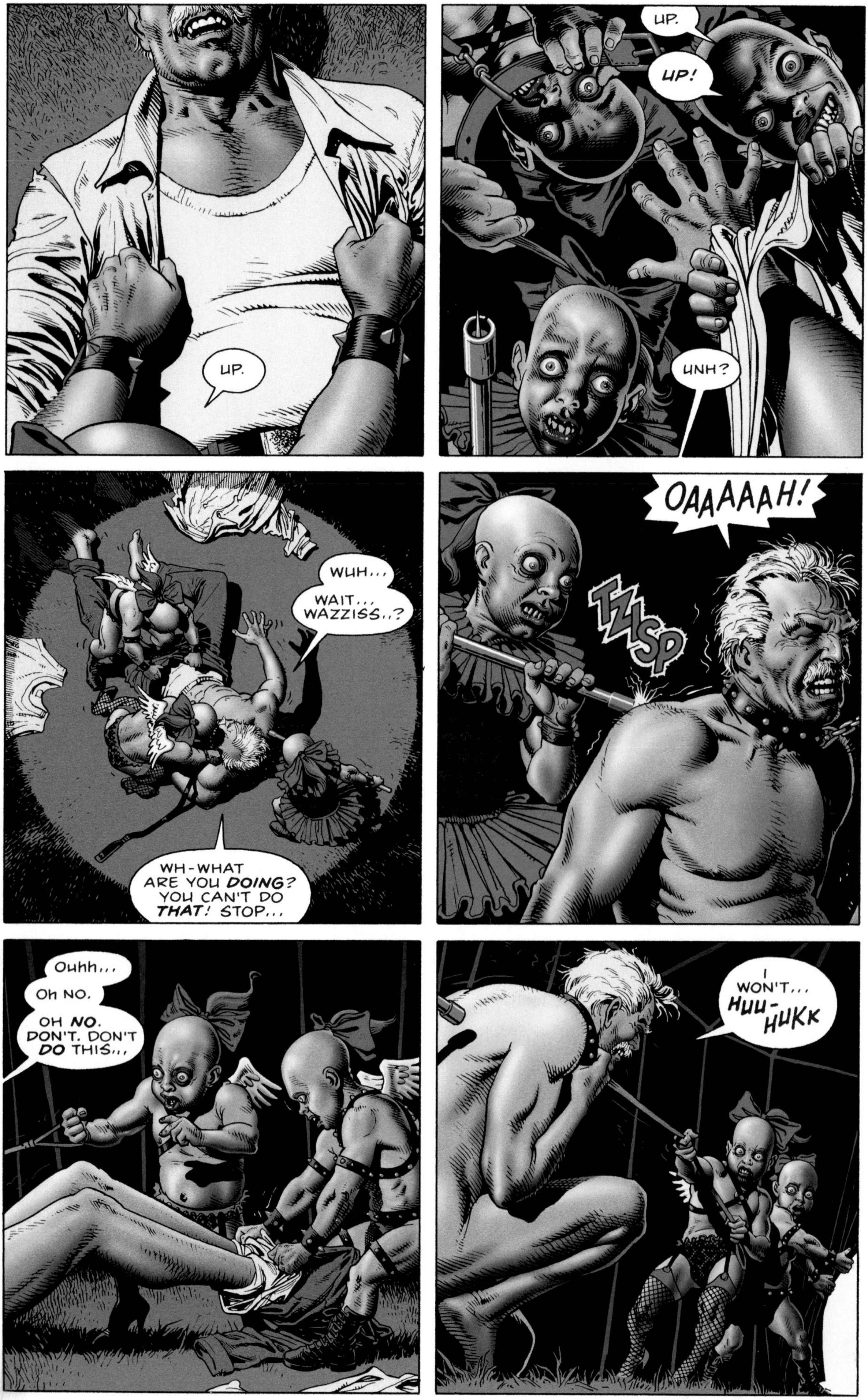
UP.
UP.
UP!
UNH?
WUH...
WAIT... WAZZISS..?
WH-WHAT ARE YOU DOING? YOU CAN'T DO THAT! STOP...
OAAAAAH!
TZISP
Ouhh...
Oh NO.
OH NO. DON'T. DON'T DO THIS...
I WON'T... HUU-HUKK

PLEASE... WHAT *IS* THIS...

WHERE ARE YOU = *hhik* = WHERE ARE YOU *TAKING* ME? I...

Oh.

OH DEAR GOD.

FUN

Oh GOD. AM I *DREAMING*? AM I *DREAMING* THIS? WHAT *HAPPENED*? I WAS SITTING IN MY...

DOWN.

WHAT?

DOWN!

UHUUUGH...

UHUUUGH. SOMEBODY... PLEASE... TELL ME WHAT I'M *DOING* HERE...

DOING?

YOU'RE DOING WHAT *ANY* SANE MAN IN YOUR *APPALLING* CIRCUMSTANCES WOULD DO.

YOU'RE GOING *MAD*.

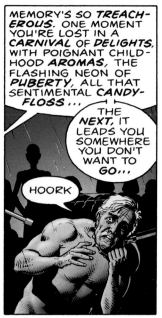

SO, EVERYTHING'S *SETTLED* FOR *TONIGHT?* YOU'RE STILL GOIN' *THROUGH* WITH IT?

UH, WELL, OF *COURSE!* I'D BE *CRAZY* TO BACK OUT *NOW.*

I MEAN, THE *WORST* PART, LYING TO *JEANNIE,* THAT'S *OVER.* SHE, SHE THINKS I HAVE A *CLUB ENGAGEMENT* TONIGHT...

NO REASON WHY SHE SHOULDN'T KEEP RIGHT ON *THINKING* THAT.

RIGHT, MAN. NO REASON AT ALL.

LISTEN: TONIGHT, WEAR A SUIT AND *BOW TIE.* IT'S A KINDA *TRADE-MARK* WITH THIS *RED HOOD* BUSINESS.

OF *COURSE!* THAT'S WHAT JEANNIE WILL *EXPECT* ME TO WEAR, FOR THE *NIGHT-CLUB.* IT'S *PERFECT!*

UH, JOE...

EXCUSE ME, SIR, WE'RE *POLICE OFFICERS.* COULD WE SPEAK TO YOU *OUTSIDE* FOR A MOMENT?

ME? B-BUT..., *WHY?* I HAVEN'T..., I MEAN, UH...

IT'LL ONLY TAKE A *MOMENT,* SIR...

UH, LISTEN, WHAT, WHAT, WHAT'S THE *PROBLEM* HERE? I...

SIR, I'M *SORRY,* BUT YOUR *WIFE* HAD AN *ACCIDENT* THIS MORNING, APPARENTLY TESTING A *BABY-BOTTLE HEATER.* THERE WAS AN *ELECTRICAL SHORT,* AND, UH...

WELL, SHE *DIED,* SIR. I'M *SORRY.*

WHAT?

LISTEN, I *HATE* TO *BREAK* IT TO YOU LIKE THIS. IT WAS A *MILLION TO ONE ACCIDENT!* THEY HAVE *FULL DETAILS* WAITING FOR YOU AT THE *HOSPITAL.*

THERE'S NO *HURRY.*

IF *I* WAS YOU, I'D HAVE ANOTHER *DRINK.*

MY WIFE. SHE'S *DEAD.* MY WIFE...

GEE, THAT'S *TERRIBLE.* WE'RE REALLY *SORRY.*

YEAH, HEY, LISTEN, MAN, YOU PROBABLY WANNA BE LEFT *ALONE* RIGHT NOW, HUH? WE'LL SEE YOU HERE *TONIGHT,* OKAY?

TONIGHT? BUT... BUT I CAN'T DO ANYTHING *TONIGHT.* TH-THERE'S NO *REASON* ANYMORE. JEANNIE... JEANNIE... JEANNIE'S *DEAD.* YOU DON'T *UNDERSTAND...*

NO, NO, NO. NO, I'M *SORRY* ABOUT YOUR *WIFE,* BUT IT'S *YOU* THAT DON'T *UNDERSTAND.*

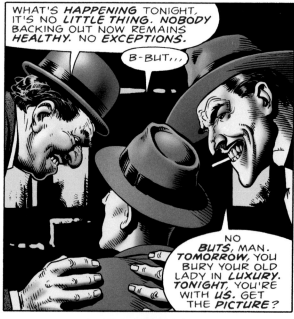

WHAT'S *HAPPENING* TONIGHT, IT'S NO *LITTLE THING. NOBODY* BACKING OUT NOW REMAINS *HEALTHY.* NO *EXCEPTIONS.*

B-BUT...

NO *BUTS,* MAN. *TOMORROW,* YOU BURY YOUR OLD LADY IN *LUXURY.* TONIGHT, YOU'RE WITH *US.* GET THE *PICTURE?*

YES. YES, I GET THE PICTURE.

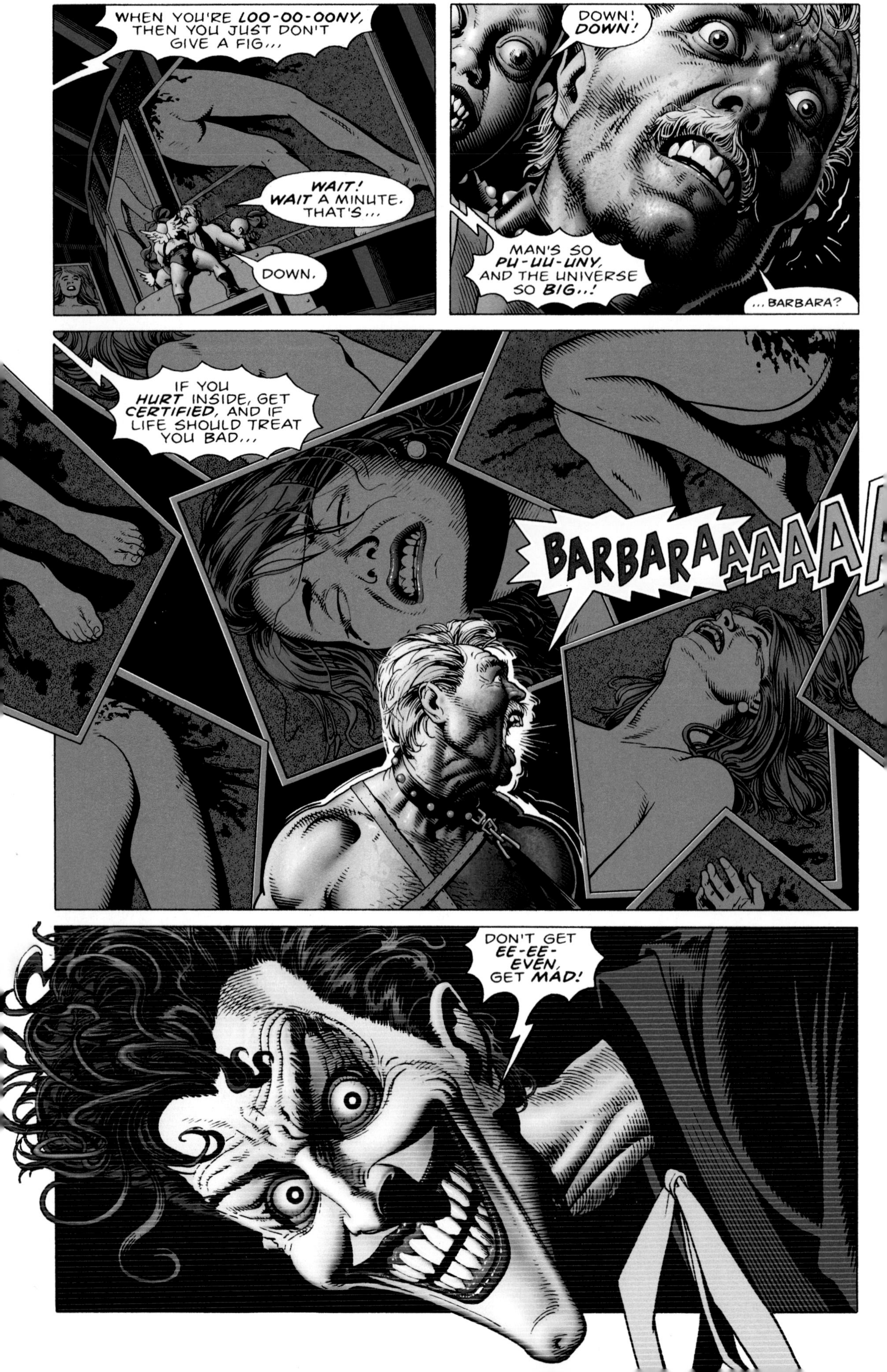

WHEN YOU'RE LOO-OO-OONY, THEN YOU JUST DON'T GIVE A FIG...
WAIT! WAIT A MINUTE. THAT'S...
DOWN.
DOWN! DOWN!
MAN'S SO PU-UU-UNY, AND THE UNIVERSE SO BIG...!
...BARBARA?
IF YOU HURT INSIDE, GET CERTIFIED, AND IF LIFE SHOULD TREAT YOU BAD...
BARBARAAAAAA
DON'T GET EE-EE-EVEN, GET MAD!

BDUMP

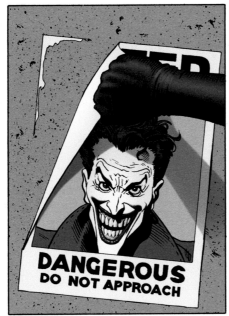

DANGEROUS
DO NOT APPROACH

BDUMP

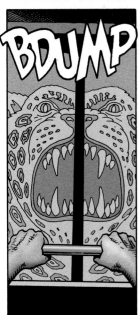

BDUMP

NO
TRUCKS

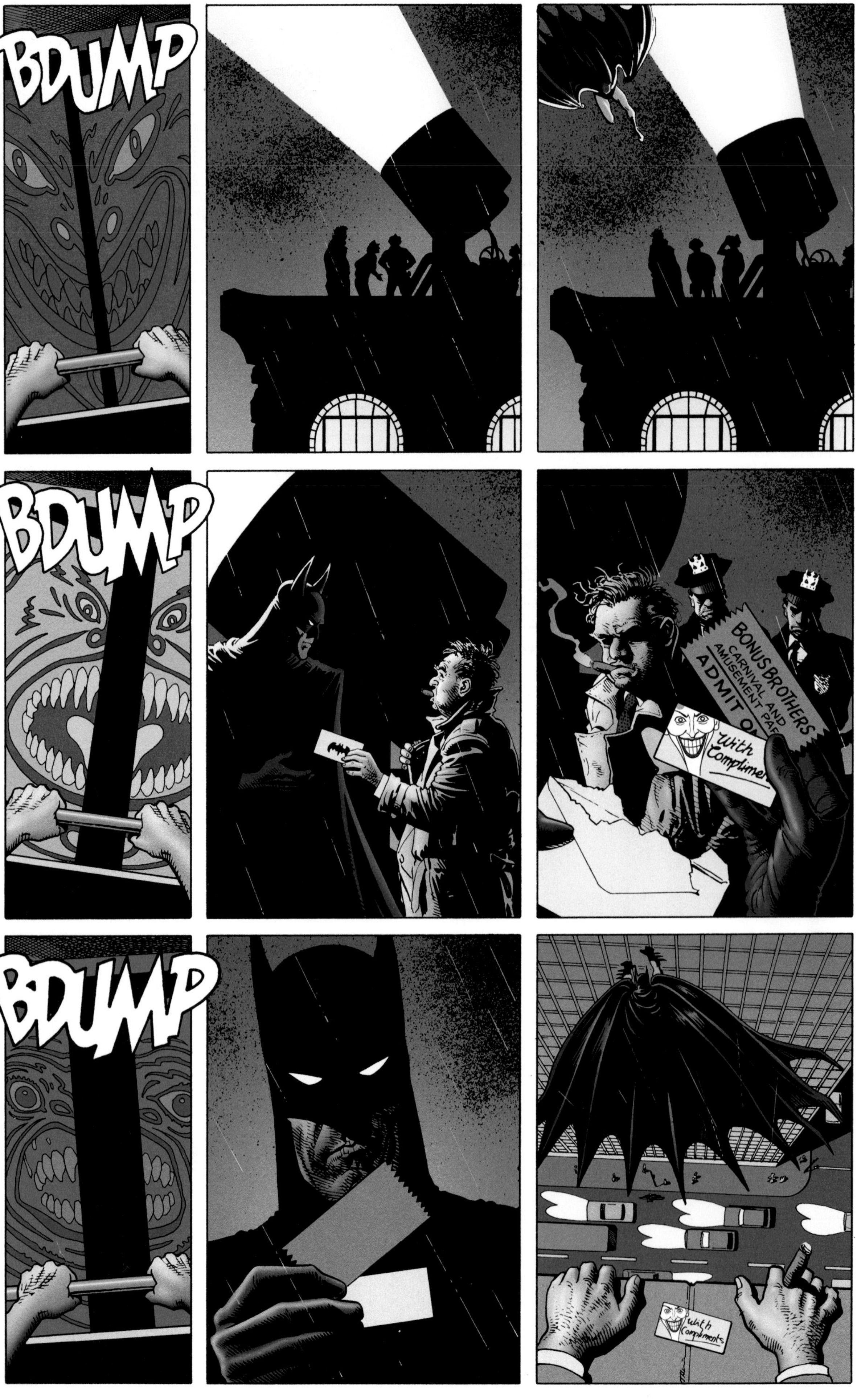
BDUMP
BDUMP
BONUS BROTHERS
CARNIVAL AND
With
BDUMP
With Compliments

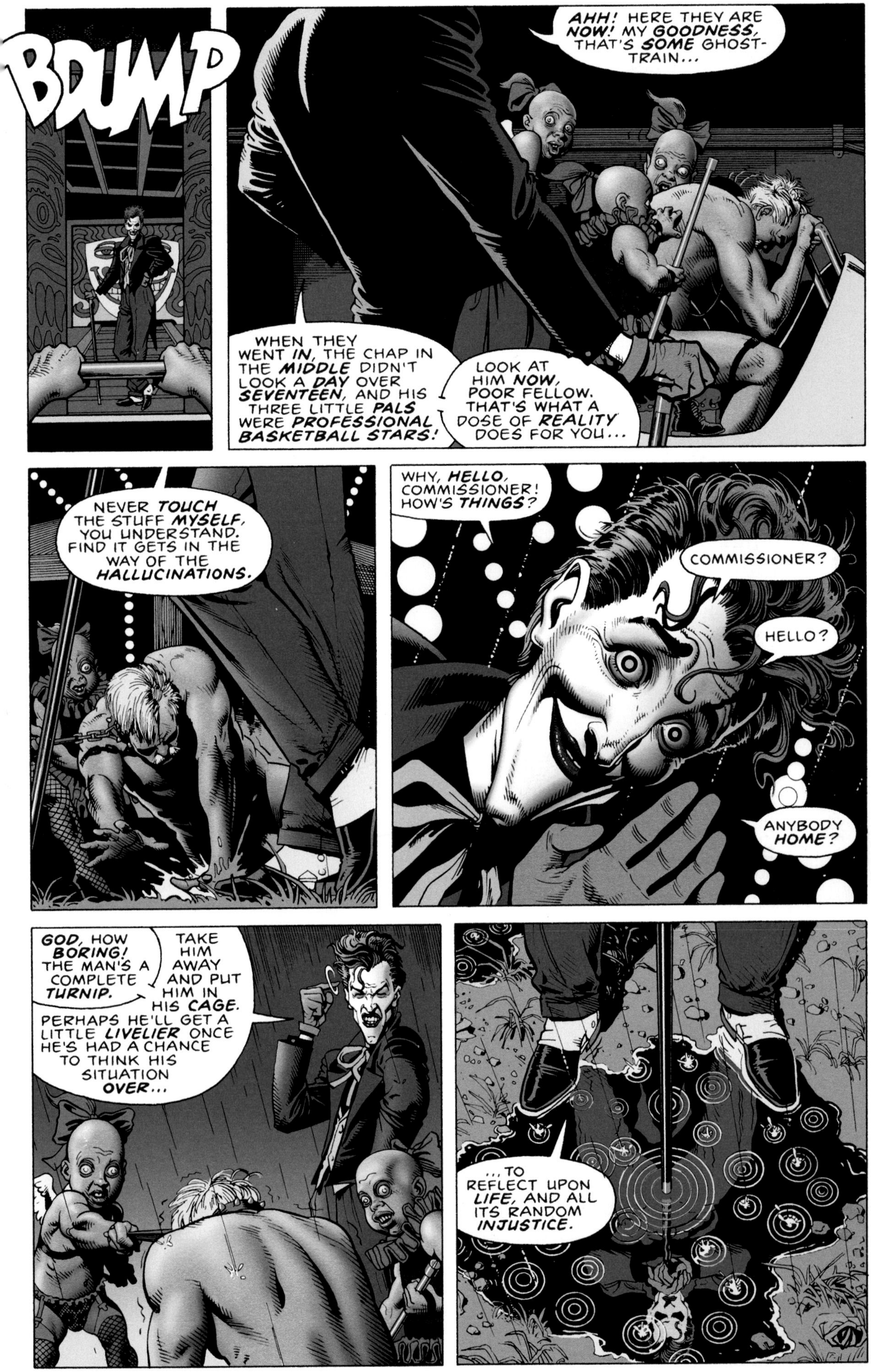
BDUMP
AHH! HERE THEY ARE NOW! MY GOODNESS, THAT'S SOME GHOST-TRAIN...
WHEN THEY WENT IN, THE CHAP IN THE MIDDLE DIDN'T LOOK A DAY OVER SEVENTEEN, AND HIS THREE LITTLE PALS WERE PROFESSIONAL BASKETBALL STARS!
LOOK AT HIM NOW, POOR FELLOW. THAT'S WHAT A DOSE OF REALITY DOES FOR YOU...
NEVER TOUCH THE STUFF MYSELF, YOU UNDERSTAND. FIND IT GETS IN THE WAY OF THE HALLUCINATIONS.
WHY, HELLO, COMMISSIONER! HOW'S THINGS?
COMMISSIONER?
HELLO?
ANYBODY HOME?
GOD, HOW BORING! THE MAN'S A COMPLETE TURNIP.
TAKE HIM AWAY AND PUT HIM IN HIS CAGE.
PERHAPS HE'LL GET A LITTLE LIVELIER ONCE HE'S HAD A CHANCE TO THINK HIS SITUATION OVER...
...TO REFLECT UPON LIFE, AND ALL ITS RANDOM INJUSTICE.

HEY, C'MON! QUIT *DAYDREAMIN'!* ARE WE *DOING* THIS THING OR AIN'T WE?

UH, YES. YES, OF *COURSE.* I WAS, I WAS JUST *REMEMBERING...* I USED TO *WALK* ALONG HERE ON THE WAY TO *WORK* EACH MORNING...

YEAH, YEAH. NOW PUT THIS SUCKER ON, MAN, AN' SHUT UP.

WHAT, RIGHT *NOW?* I MEAN... I MEAN, ARE YOU *SURE* IT'S *OKAY?*

WILL I BE ABLE TO *BREATHE?*

HEY, MAN, EVERYTHING'S *COOL.* JEEZ... Y'KNOW, YOU GOT A FUNNY-SHAPED *HEAD...*

THERE. YOU STILL SEE OKAY, MAN?

WUH, WELL, YEAH. I GUESS, EXCEPT EVERY-THING'S *RED...* IT'S KINDA *STUFFY* TOO, AND IT *SMELLS* FUNNY. DOES MY VOICE SOUND *ECHOEY* TO YOU?

YOU SOUND *GREAT.* NOW... HOW ABOUT *GUIDIN'* US THROUGH THIS STINKIN' *FACTORY* TO THE JOINT NEXT *DOOR?*

SURE. SURE THING, Y'KNOW... THIS FEELS KINDA *WEIRD.* LIKE A *DREAM.* I KEEP REMEMBERING *JEANNIE...*

WATCH *OUT,* MAN. STEPS.

OKAY... WE GO THROUGH *HERE,* PAST THE *FILTER TANKS* AND THEN *MONARCH PLAYING CARDS* IS JUST BEYOND A *PARTITION.*

Y'KNOW, THIS PLACE... IT LOOKS EVEN *WORSE* IN *RED.* IT LOOKS LIKE...

HEY, YOU! *FREEEEEZE!*

C'MON, C'MON, GET 'EM *UP!*

YOU *ASSHOLE!* YOU SAID THERE WAS NO *SECURITY!*

THEY... THEY MUST HAVE *ALTERED THINGS* SINCE I *LEFT...*

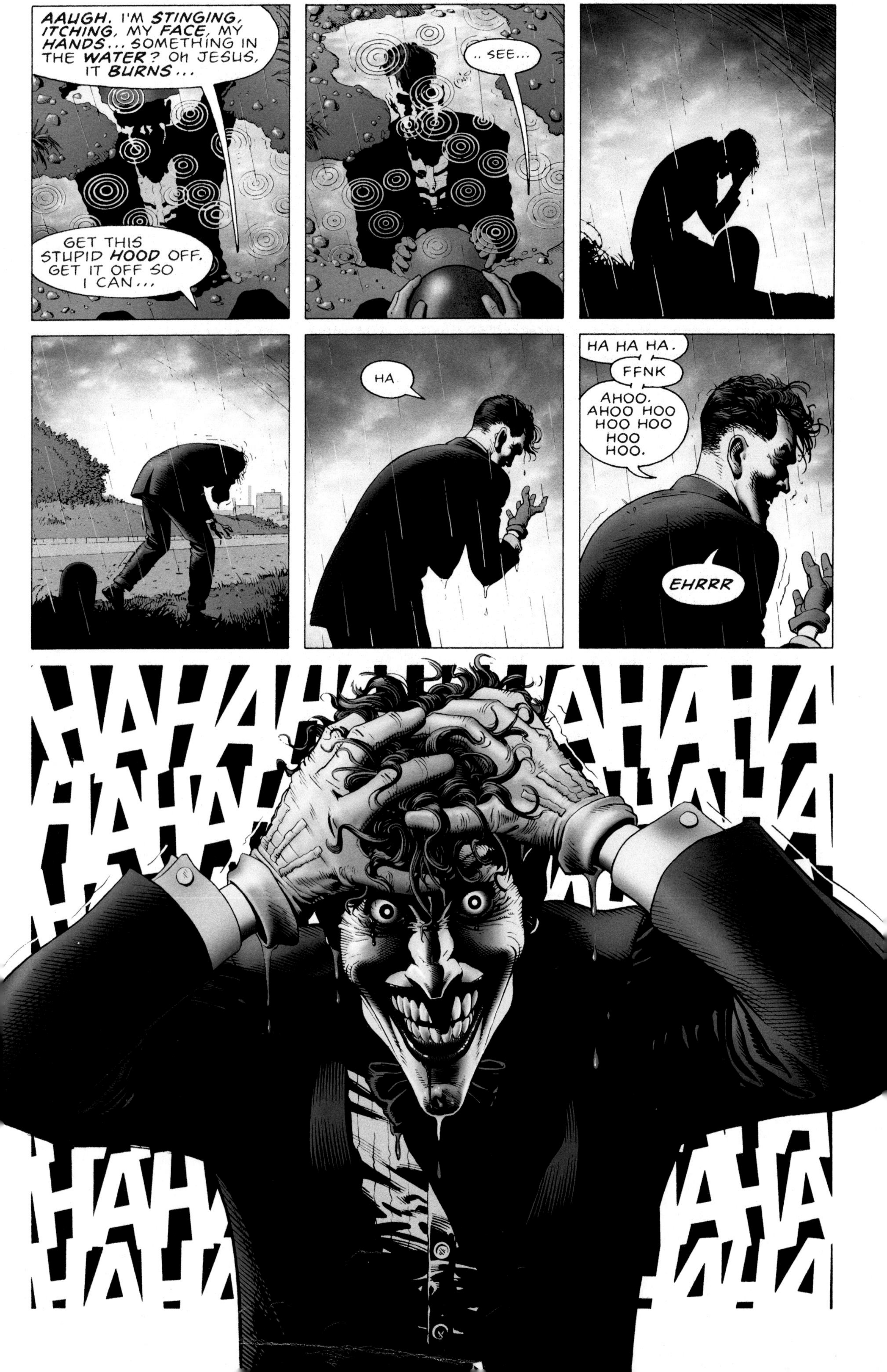
AAUGH. I'M STINGING, ITCHING, MY FACE, MY HANDS... SOMETHING IN THE WATER? Oh JESUS, IT BURNS...
GET THIS STUPID HOOD OFF. GET IT OFF SO I CAN...
.. SEE...
HA
HA HA HA.
FFNK
AHOO. AHOO HOO HOO HOO HOO HOO.
EHRRR
HAHAHAHAHAHAHA

AHIHIHIHIHI... AHIHIHIHIHI.

THAT'S SO FUNNY.

THAT'S SO FUNNY.

AUF! HA-AUFF!

LADIES AND GENTLEMEN! YOU'VE READ ABOUT IT IN THE NEWSPAPERS! NOW, SHUDDER AS YOU OBSERVE, BEFORE YOUR VERY EYES, THAT MOST RARE AND TRAGIC OF NATURE'S MISTAKES!

I GIVE YOU... THE AVERAGE MAN!

OOUHH...

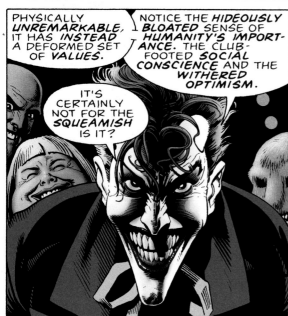

PHYSICALLY UNREMARKABLE, IT HAS INSTEAD A DEFORMED SET OF VALUES.

NOTICE THE HIDEOUSLY BLOATED SENSE OF HUMANITY'S IMPORTANCE. THE CLUB-FOOTED SOCIAL CONSCIENCE AND THE WITHERED OPTIMISM.

IT'S CERTAINLY NOT FOR THE SQUEAMISH IS IT?

MOST REPULSIVE OF ALL, ARE ITS FRAIL AND USELESS NOTIONS OF ORDER AND SANITY. IF TOO MUCH WEIGHT IS PLACED UPON THEM...

...THEY SNAP.

HOW DOES IT LIVE, I HEAR YOU ASK?

HOW DOES THIS POOR, PATHETIC SPECIMEN SURVIVE IN TODAY'S HARSH AND IRRATIONAL WORLD?

THE SAD ANSWER IS "NOT VERY WELL."

FACED WITH THE INESCAPABLE FACT THAT HUMAN EXISTENCE IS MAD, RANDOM AND POINTLESS, ONE IN EIGHT OF THEM CRACK UP AND GO STARK SLAVERING BUGGO!

WHO CAN BLAME THEM? IN A WORLD AS PSYCHOTIC AS THIS...

...ANY OTHER RESPONSE WOULD BE CRAZY!

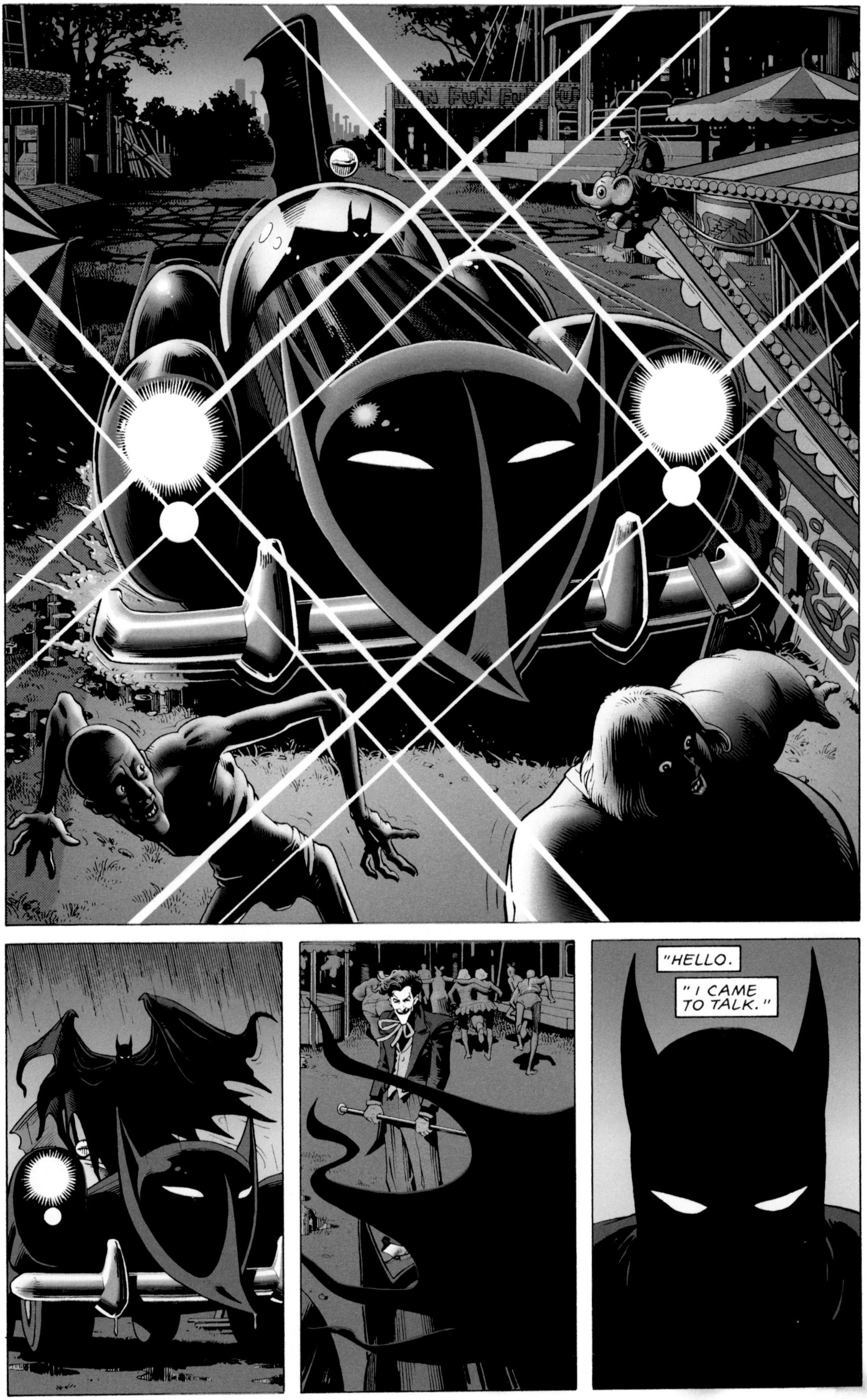
"HELLO.
"I CAME TO TALK."

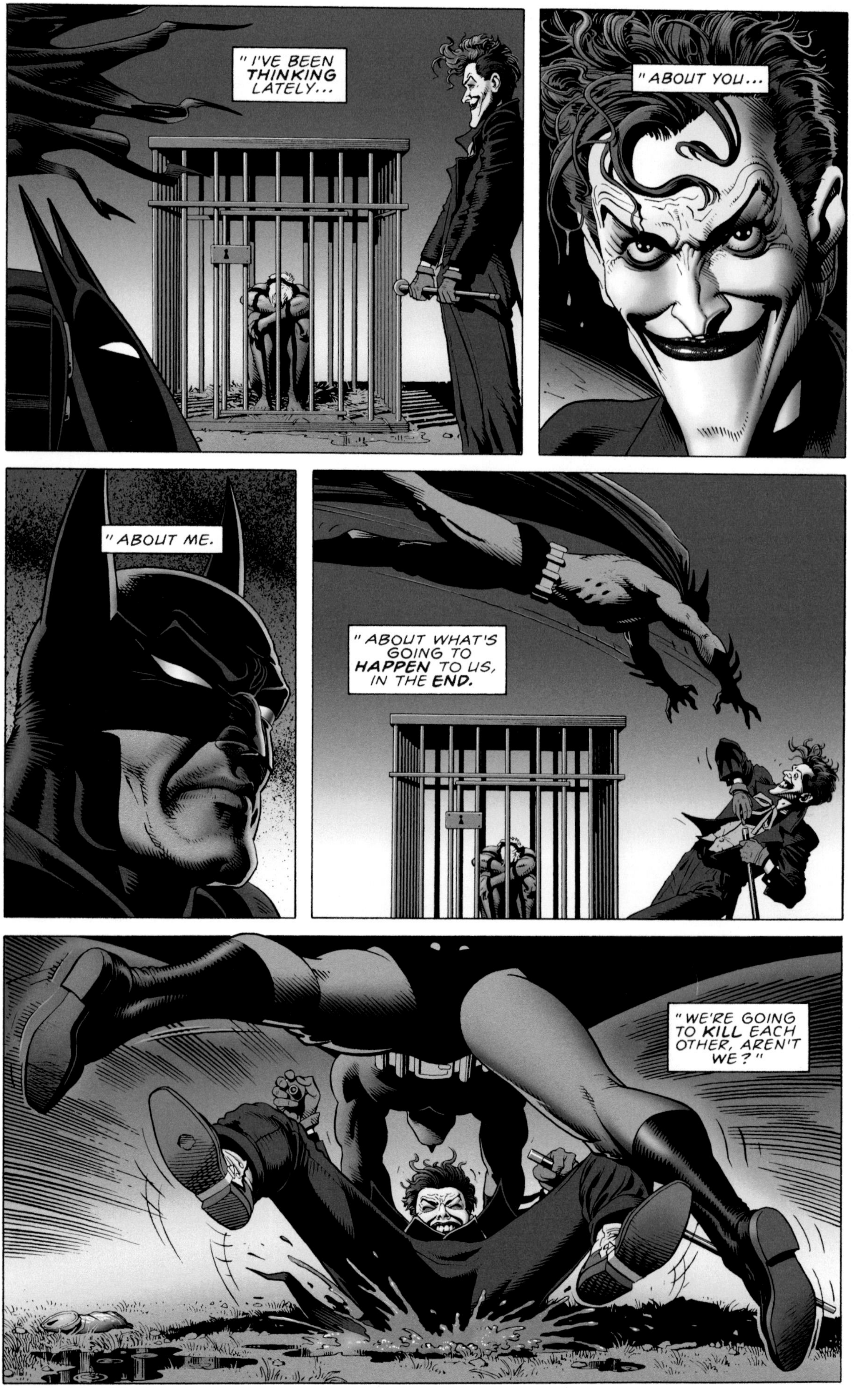
"I'VE BEEN THINKING LATELY...
"ABOUT YOU...
"ABOUT ME.
"ABOUT WHAT'S GOING TO HAPPEN TO US, IN THE END.
"WE'RE GOING TO KILL EACH OTHER, AREN'T WE?"

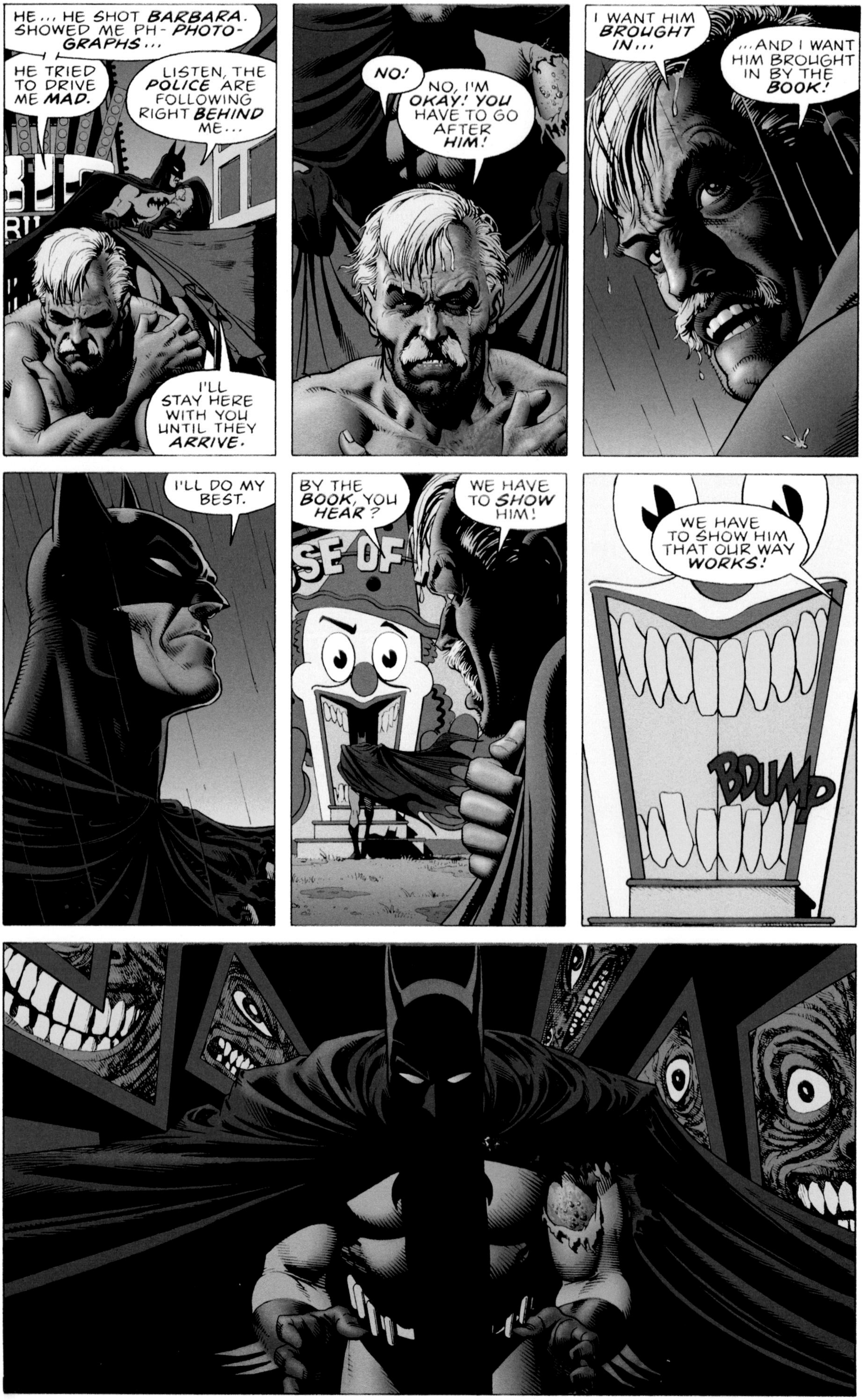
HE... HE SHOT BARBARA. SHOWED ME PH-PHOTOGRAPHS...
HE TRIED TO DRIVE ME MAD.
LISTEN, THE POLICE ARE FOLLOWING RIGHT BEHIND ME...
I'LL STAY HERE WITH YOU UNTIL THEY ARRIVE.
NO!
NO, I'M OKAY! YOU HAVE TO GO AFTER HIM!
I WANT HIM BROUGHT IN...
...AND I WANT HIM BROUGHT IN BY THE BOOK!
I'LL DO MY BEST.
BY THE BOOK, YOU HEAR?
WE HAVE TO SHOW HIM!
WE HAVE TO SHOW HIM THAT OUR WAY WORKS!
BDUMP

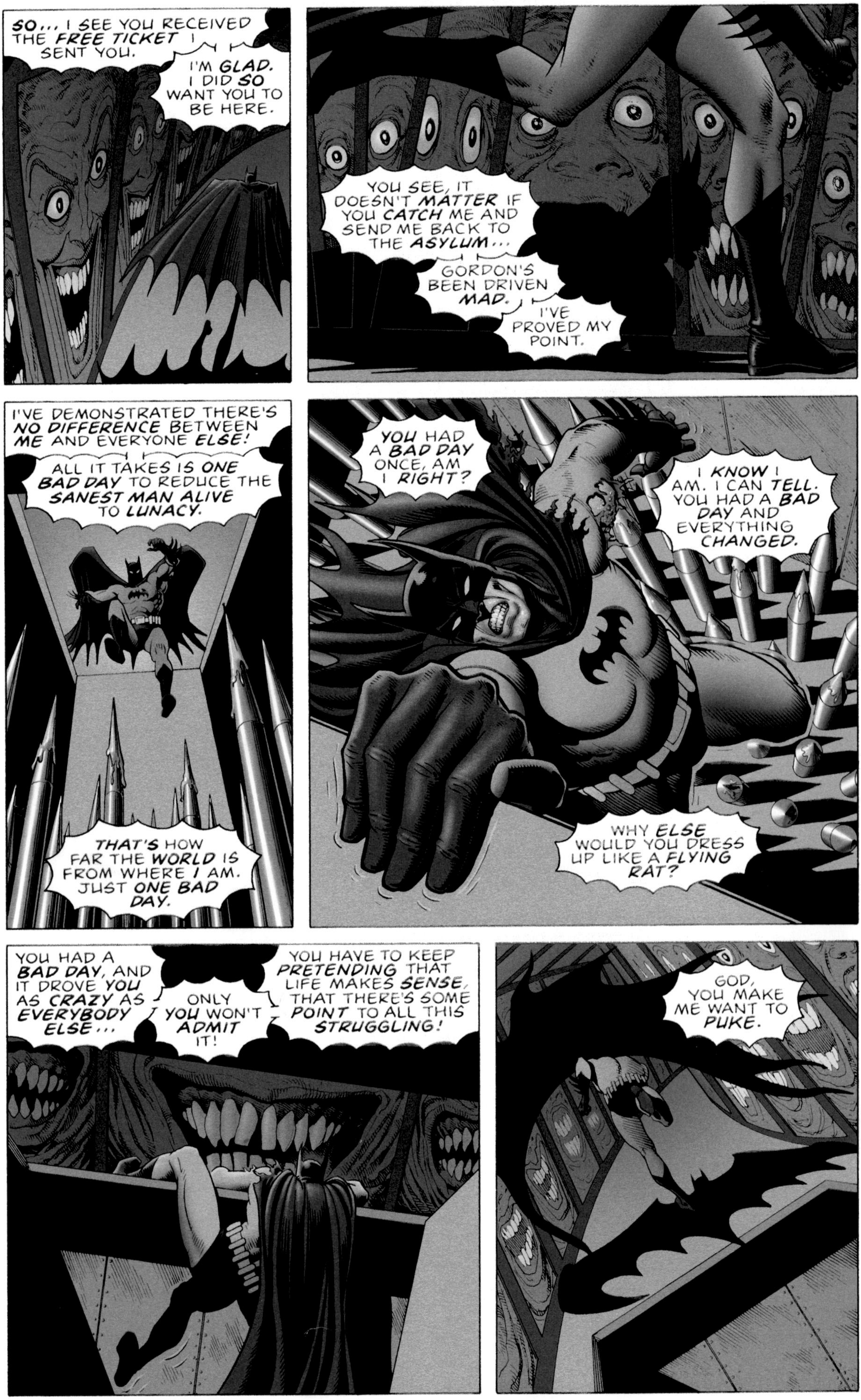
SO... I SEE YOU RECEIVED THE FREE TICKET I SENT YOU.
I'M GLAD. I DID SO WANT YOU TO BE HERE.
YOU SEE, IT DOESN'T MATTER IF YOU CATCH ME AND SEND ME BACK TO THE ASYLUM...
GORDON'S BEEN DRIVEN MAD.
I'VE PROVED MY POINT.
I'VE DEMONSTRATED THERE'S NO DIFFERENCE BETWEEN ME AND EVERYONE ELSE!
ALL IT TAKES IS ONE BAD DAY TO REDUCE THE SANEST MAN ALIVE TO LUNACY.
THAT'S HOW FAR THE WORLD IS FROM WHERE I AM. JUST ONE BAD DAY.
YOU HAD A BAD DAY ONCE, AM I RIGHT?
I KNOW I AM. I CAN TELL. YOU HAD A BAD DAY AND EVERYTHING CHANGED.
WHY ELSE WOULD YOU DRESS UP LIKE A FLYING RAT?
YOU HAD A BAD DAY, AND IT DROVE YOU AS CRAZY AS EVERYBODY ELSE...
ONLY YOU WON'T ADMIT IT!
YOU HAVE TO KEEP PRETENDING THAT LIFE MAKES SENSE, THAT THERE'S SOME POINT TO ALL THIS STRUGGLING!
GOD, YOU MAKE ME WANT TO PUKE.

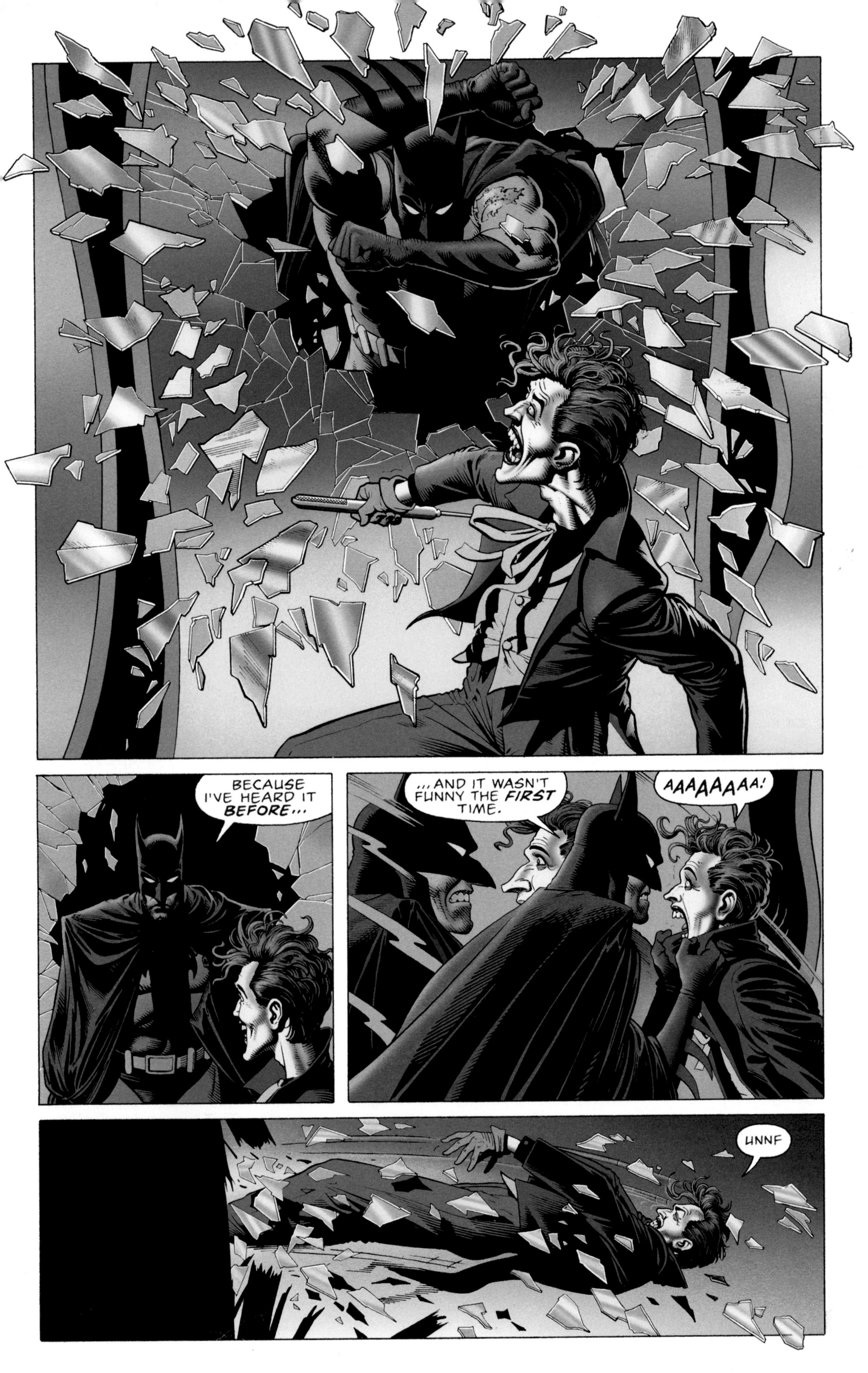
BECAUSE I'VE HEARD IT BEFORE...
...AND IT WASN'T FUNNY THE FIRST TIME.
AAAAAAAA!
UNNF

INCIDENTALLY, I *SPOKE* TO COMMISSIONER GORDON BEFORE I CAME *IN* HERE. HE'S *FINE*.

DESPITE ALL YOUR SICK, VICIOUS, LITTLE *GAMES*, HE'S AS *SANE* AS HE *EVER* WAS.

SO MAYBE ORDINARY PEOPLE *DON'T* ALWAYS CRACK.

GAAAK

MAYBE THERE *ISN'T* ANY NEED TO CRAWL UNDER A *ROCK* WITH ALL THE *OTHER* SLIMEY THINGS WHEN TROUBLE HITS...

MAYBE IT WAS *YOU*, ALL THE TIME.

NO!

UNNGH

DON'T...

AHAH! AHAH!

HHUT

NNMF

GNUHHH...

FTCHK!

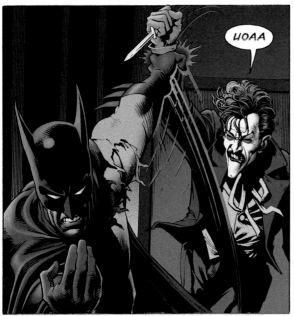

UOAA

HOOOF

FUHHH...

BDUMP

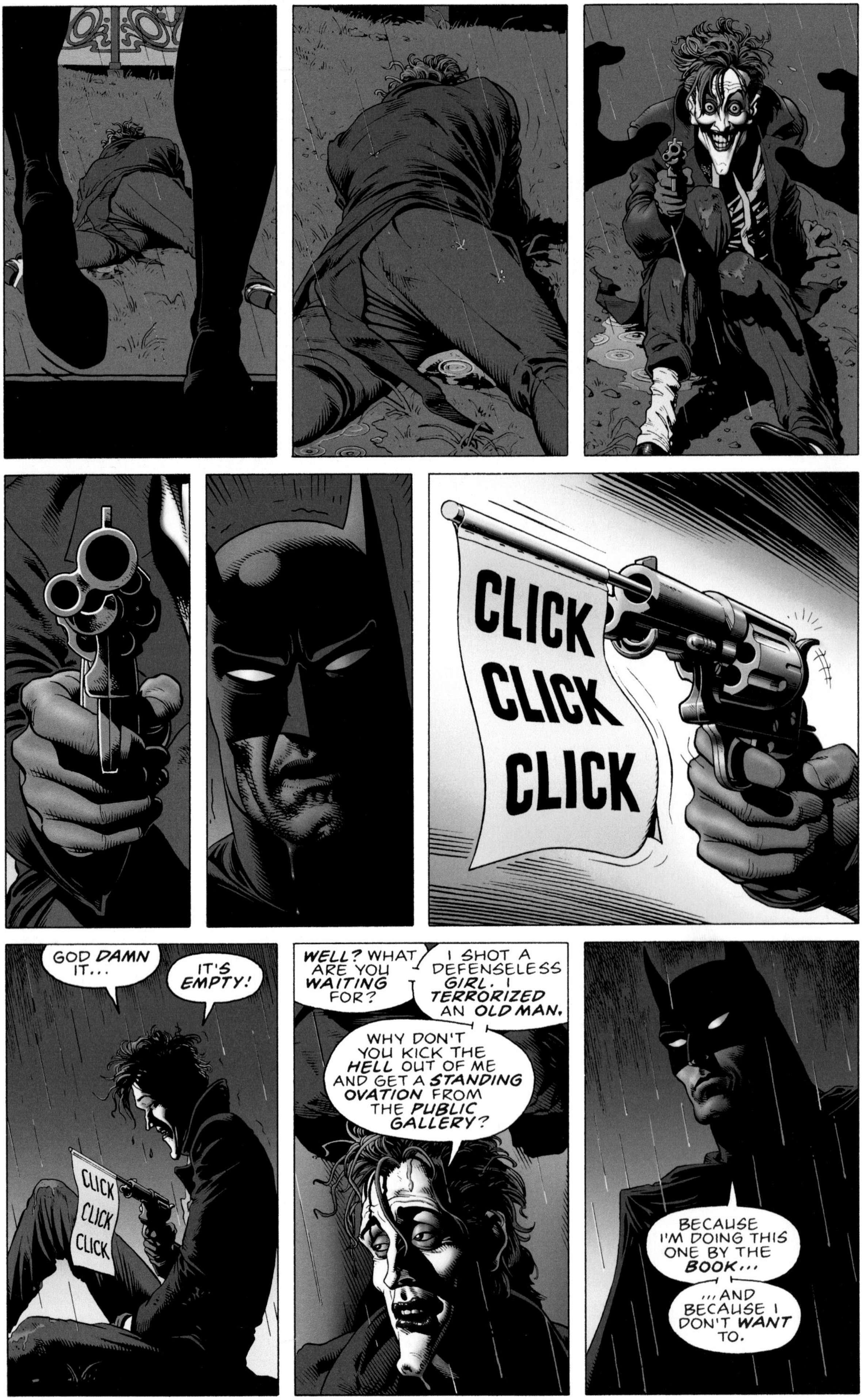
CLICK
CLICK
CLICK
GOD DAMN IT...
IT'S EMPTY!
CLICK
CLICK
CLICK
WELL? WHAT ARE YOU WAITING FOR?
I SHOT A DEFENSELESS GIRL. I TERRORIZED AN OLD MAN.
WHY DON'T YOU KICK THE HELL OUT OF ME AND GET A STANDING OVATION FROM THE PUBLIC GALLERY?
BECAUSE I'M DOING THIS ONE BY THE BOOK...
...AND BECAUSE I DON'T WANT TO.

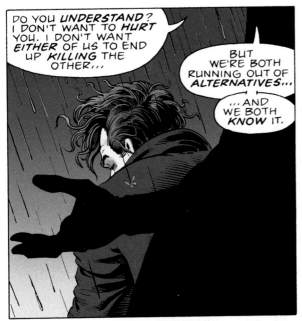

DO YOU *UNDERSTAND?* I DON'T WANT TO *HURT* YOU. I DON'T WANT *EITHER* OF US TO END UP *KILLING* THE OTHER...

BUT WE'RE BOTH RUNNING OUT OF *ALTERNATIVES*...

...AND WE BOTH *KNOW* IT.

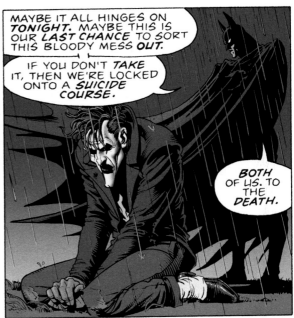

MAYBE IT ALL HINGES ON *TONIGHT.* MAYBE THIS IS OUR *LAST CHANCE* TO SORT THIS BLOODY MESS *OUT.*

IF YOU DON'T *TAKE* IT, THEN WE'RE LOCKED ONTO A *SUICIDE COURSE.*

BOTH OF US. TO THE *DEATH.*

IT DOESN'T *HAVE* TO END LIKE THAT. I DON'T KNOW WHAT IT *WAS* THAT BENT YOUR *LIFE* OUT OF *SHAPE,* BUT WHO *KNOWS?*

MAYBE I'VE BEEN THERE *TOO.*

MAYBE I CAN *HELP.*

WE COULD *WORK* TOGETHER. I COULD *REHABILITATE* YOU. YOU NEEDN'T BE OUT THERE ON THE *EDGE* ANY MORE. YOU NEEDN'T BE *ALONE.*

WE DON'T *HAVE* TO KILL EACH OTHER.

WHAT DO YOU *SAY?*

NO. I'M SORRY, BUT...

NO. IT'S TOO *LATE* FOR THAT. *FAR* TOO LATE.

HAHAHA. Y'KNOW, IT'S *FUNNY*... THIS *SITUATION.* IT REMINDS ME OF A *JOKE*...

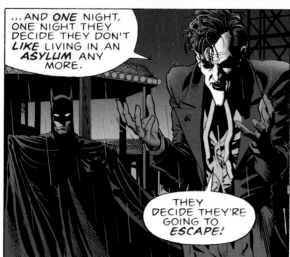

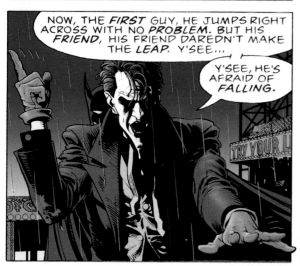

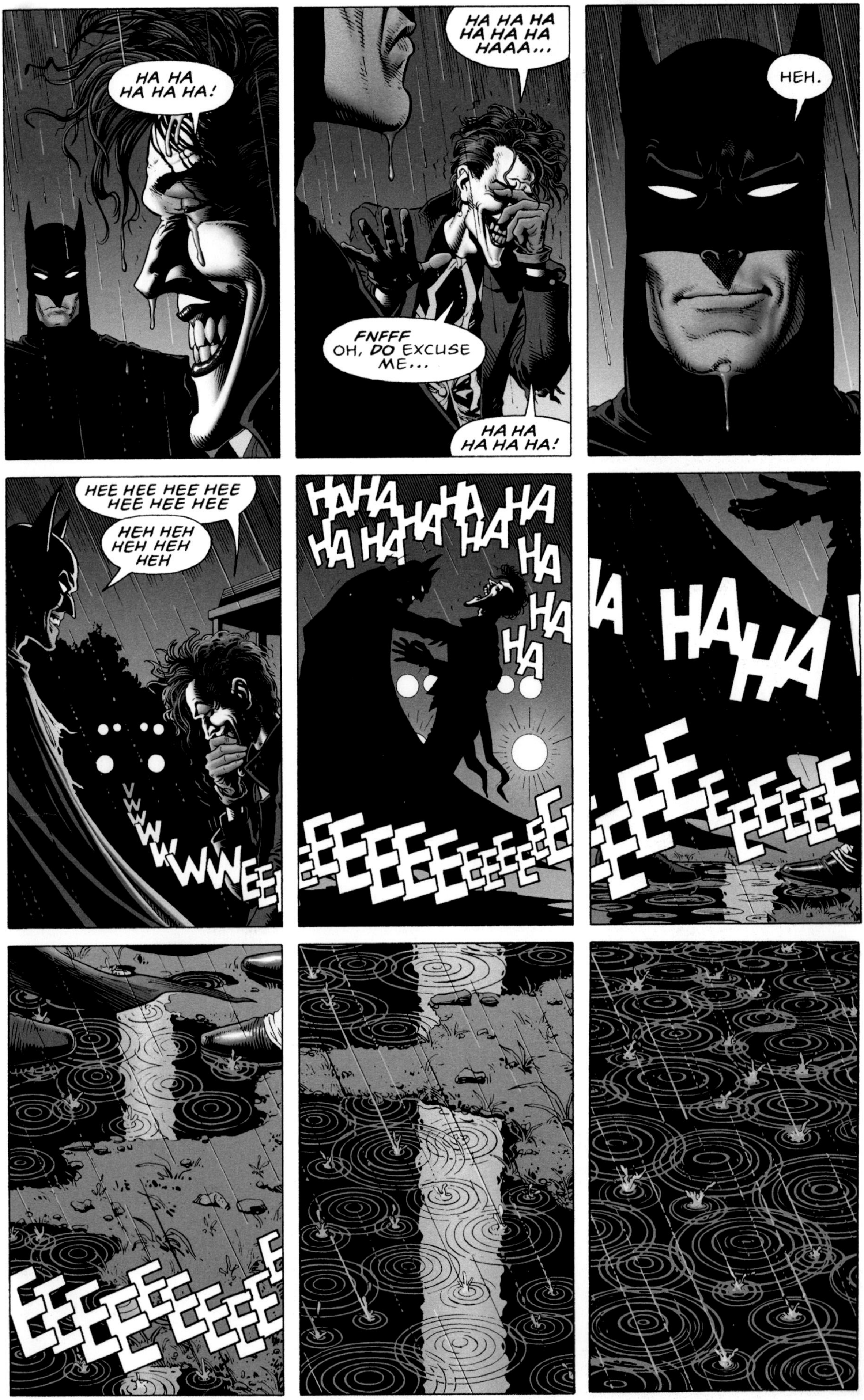
HA HA HA HA HA!
HA HA HA HA HA HA HAAA...
FNFFF OH, DO EXCUSE ME...
HA HA HA HA HA!
HEH.
HEE HEE HEE HEE HEE HEE HEE
HEH HEH HEH HEH HEH
WWWWWEEE
HA HA HA HA HA HA HA HA HA HA HA HA HA
EEEEEEEEEEEEEEEEEE
HAHA
EEEEEEEEEEE
EEEEEEEEEEEE

AFTERWORD

I've been asked to write the "afterword" to this book —
or should that be the "in between"? I'm told by my
editor Bob Harras that there's room for up to 800
words. If I go on longer we have to start dropping
pages of art and we wouldn't want that, would we? So,
reader, if I should stop in mid-sentence it's because
I've run out of space.

I've just read Tim Sale's generous introduction. Of all
the introductions I've ever received, it's without doubt
the most....recent. Having just sat with my 11-year old
son watching the hit TV show *Heroes*, it's pretty cool
being introduced by its star artist. It seems addition-
ally cool to me that all the writing in this book has
been given over not to writers but to artists, a breed of
people not known for their ability to string a sentence
together — but so far so good.

There's a minor detail that Tim got wrong, actually. It
was me that asked Alan to write the book and not the
other way round. THE KILLING JOKE was not a project
instigated by Alan, nor was it, as far as I know, a labor
of love for him, and it doesn't usually appear in a list
of his greatest works. I was glad he agreed to write it,
though. At the time we'd known each other for quite a
while and narrowly missed working together a couple
of times. In a peculiar form of homage to him I haven't
drawn a comic book story written by any other writer
in the last 22 years. When you've worked with the best,
anything else would seem like a backward step.

The script for THE KILLING JOKE was very good, but I must admit I had to grit my teeth a couple of times during the drawing of it. I, for instance, would never have chosen to reveal a Joker origin. I think of this as just one of a number of possible origin stories manifesting itself in the Joker's fevered brain. Also, I wouldn't have done such terrible harm to poor Barbara. The story, though, does contain some great iconic moments, my favorite being the scene when the Joker discovers that the gun — as far as we know the same one that maimed Barbara — is empty. People seemed to find the last page of the story ambiguous, so before I conclude this text, remind me to reveal what actually happened.

The most notable absentee from this edition is THE KILLING JOKE's original colorist, John Higgins, and I want to thank him for jumping in when he did and finishing the book so promptly. Back in the pre-computer days of "blue line," airbrush and poster colors, even though I had specific views on how I wanted it to look, I wouldn't have been able to color it myself. It's probably well known that John's choice of colors turned out to be startlingly at odds with what I had in mind so, in February 2007, when Bob Harras told me about this edition, I said, "PLEASE can I recolor the whole thing?"

Technical wizard Jeb Woodard sent me files of the line art which, through some computer alchemy only he understands, he'd isolated from the printed color pages — the original KILLING JOKE artwork has long since disappeared into the hands of collectors — and as I got on with the coloring process on my Mac it was tempting and easy to make changes to the line art itself — a bit of feathering here, a completely redrawn face there. The eagle-eyed may notice that every page has something slightly different on it from THE KILLING JOKE of 20 years ago. There's at least one figure that wasn't there the first time around. Think of it as a Spot-the-Difference book.

"An Innocent Guy" (that's what it's called even though it doesn't say so on it) is of special significance to me. As I became less inclined to work with writers or colorists it was particularly tempting to write a Batman story that was, for better or worse, completely by me. It gave me the opportunity to draw all the scenes I hadn't had a chance to draw in THE KILLING JOKE, including my homage to the unsettlingly surreal Dick Sprang-era Batman that I loved as a kid but combine it with a darker, more morally ambiguous theme that I'd stolen shamelessly from other sources. In so doing I managed to upset at least one mother of a seven-year-old boy who wrote me a letter of protest. Jeb supervised the meticulous painting out of the Zipatone that covered the artwork for the original black and white printing (he didn't quite get it all. You'll see bits of it lingering here and there) and I colored it up for the first time ever. I hope you enjoy these and the preceding 46 pages.

Speaking of which, it's time I revealed what really happened at the end of THE KILLING JOKE: as our protagonists stood there in the rain laughing at the final joke, the police lights reflecting in the pools of filthy water underfoot, the Batman's hand reached out and......

Brian Bolland

Not far from Six Mile Bottom, UK 2008

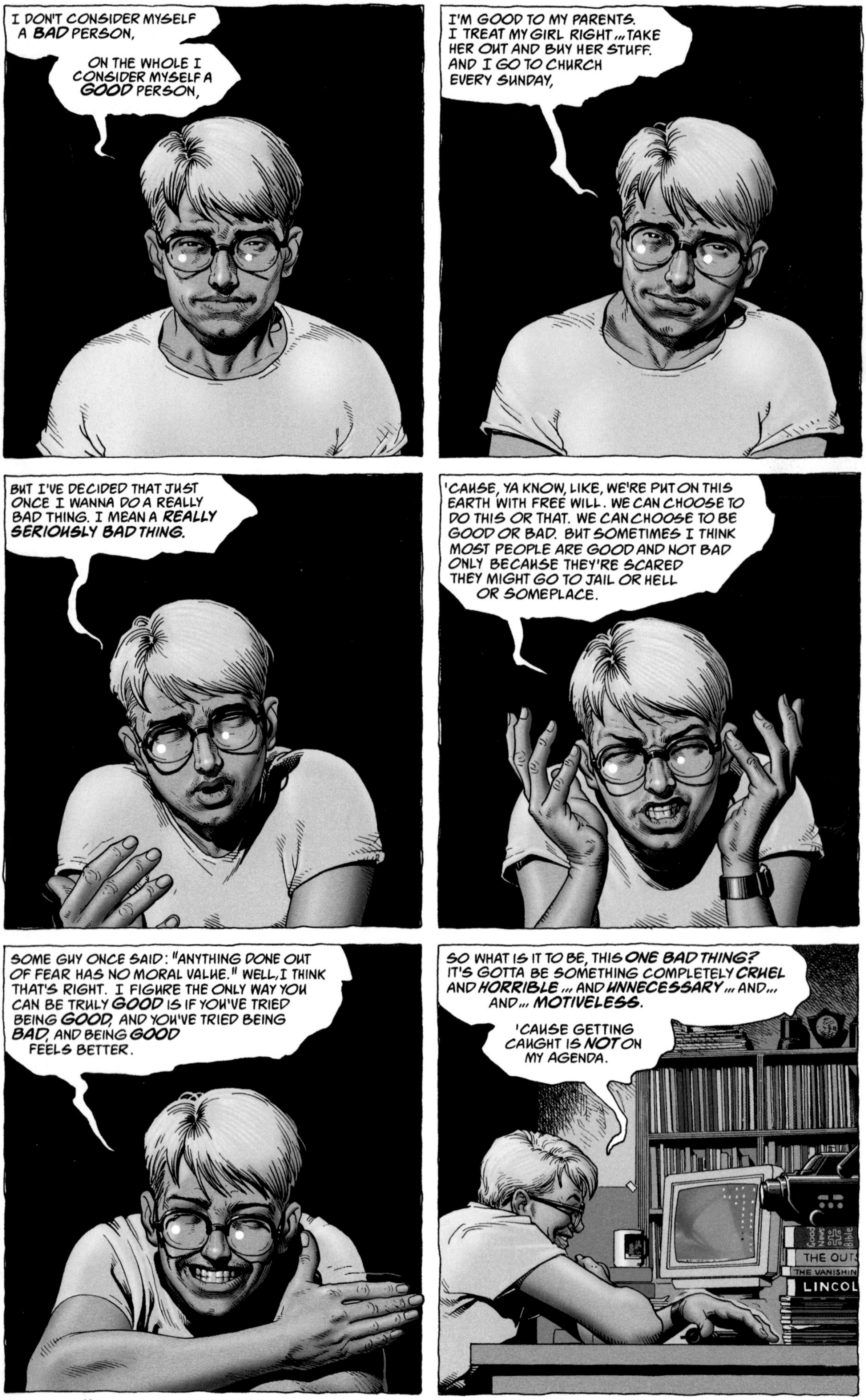
I DON'T CONSIDER MYSELF A BAD PERSON.
ON THE WHOLE I CONSIDER MYSELF A GOOD PERSON.
I'M GOOD TO MY PARENTS. I TREAT MY GIRL RIGHT... TAKE HER OUT AND BUY HER STUFF. AND I GO TO CHURCH EVERY SUNDAY.
BUT I'VE DECIDED THAT JUST ONCE I WANNA DO A REALLY BAD THING. I MEAN A REALLY SERIOUSLY BAD THING.
'CAUSE, YA KNOW, LIKE, WE'RE PUT ON THIS EARTH WITH FREE WILL. WE CAN CHOOSE TO DO THIS OR THAT. WE CAN CHOOSE TO BE GOOD OR BAD. BUT SOMETIMES I THINK MOST PEOPLE ARE GOOD AND NOT BAD ONLY BECAUSE THEY'RE SCARED THEY MIGHT GO TO JAIL OR HELL OR SOMEPLACE.
SOME GUY ONCE SAID: "ANYTHING DONE OUT OF FEAR HAS NO MORAL VALUE." WELL, I THINK THAT'S RIGHT. I FIGURE THE ONLY WAY YOU CAN BE TRULY GOOD IS IF YOU'VE TRIED BEING GOOD, AND YOU'VE TRIED BEING BAD, AND BEING GOOD FEELS BETTER.
SO WHAT IS IT TO BE, THIS ONE BAD THING? IT'S GOTTA BE SOMETHING COMPLETELY CRUEL AND HORRIBLE... AND UNNECESSARY... AND... AND... MOTIVELESS.
'CAUSE GETTING CAUGHT IS NOT ON MY AGENDA.
Good News Bible
THE OUTS
THE VANISHIN
LINCOL

Writer & Illustrator: Brian Bolland

Letterer: Ellie DeVille

THERE'S AN OLD DISUSED SEWER SHAFT OUT IN A PLACE I KNOW WHERE NO ONE EVER GOES.

I THOUGHT I'D KIDNAP A LITTLE GIRL AND CHAIN HER UP DOWN THERE AND LEAVE HER THERE WEEPING AND WAILING IN THE DARK TILL SHE STARVED TO DEATH.

YA GOTTA UNDERSTAND I'M NOT SOME KIND OF *PERVERT* OR ANYTHING LIKE THAT, BUT WHATEVER I CAN DO TO MAKE HER ORDEAL WORSE AND RUIN THE LIVES OF HER FAMILY, I'LL DO.

BUT SOMEHOW THIS *ISN'T ENOUGH.*

IT'S GOTTA BE A *BIGGER* THING SOMEHOW. SOMETHING THAT'LL LEAVE A MARK ON MORE PEOPLE LIKE THE KILLING OF *JOHN LENNON.* IT'S GOTTA BE SOMEBODY *FAMOUS.*

I THOUGHT ABOUT *THE POPE.* BUT HE'S ALWAYS SURROUNDED BY THOSE SECRET SERVICE GUYS AND RIDIN' AROUND IN HIS BULLETPROOF POPEMOBILE,

AN', WELL, I DON'T GET OVER TO *ITALY* VERY OFTEN ... IN FACT *NEVER.*

I'VE GOTTA CHOOSE MY VICTIM FOR THE SAKE OF *CONVENIENCE.* IT'S GOTTA BE SOMEONE WHO DOESN'T HAVE AN ARMED GUARD. SOMEONE RIGHT HERE IN *GOTHAM.*

IT'S GOTTA BE *THE BATMAN.*

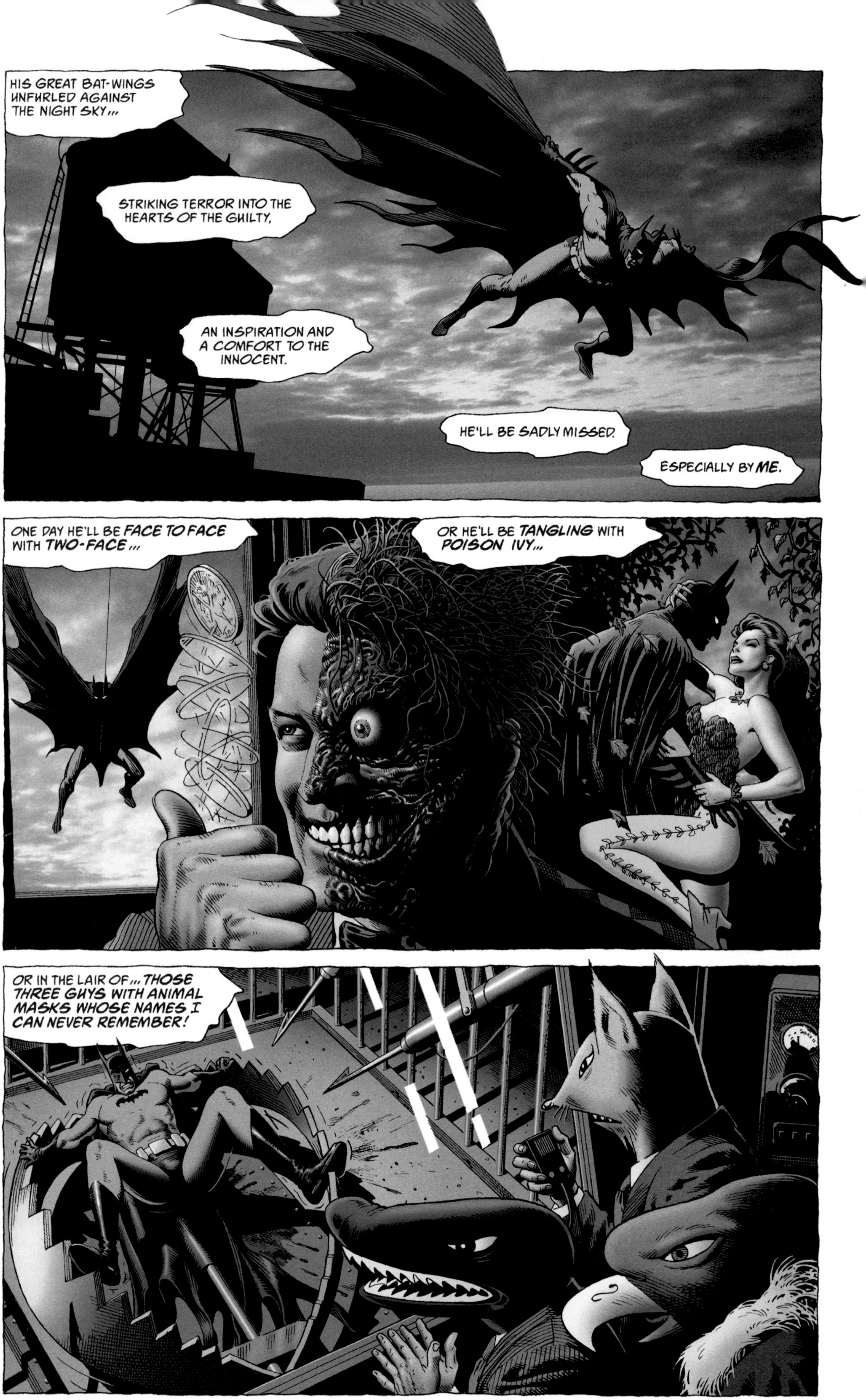
HIS GREAT BAT-WINGS UNFURLED AGAINST THE NIGHT SKY...
STRIKING TERROR INTO THE HEARTS OF THE GUILTY,
AN INSPIRATION AND A COMFORT TO THE INNOCENT.
HE'LL BE SADLY MISSED.
ESPECIALLY BY ME.
ONE DAY HE'LL BE FACE TO FACE WITH TWO-FACE...
OR HE'LL BE TANGLING WITH POISON IVY...
OR IN THE LAIR OF... THOSE THREE GUYS WITH ANIMAL MASKS WHOSE NAMES I CAN NEVER REMEMBER!

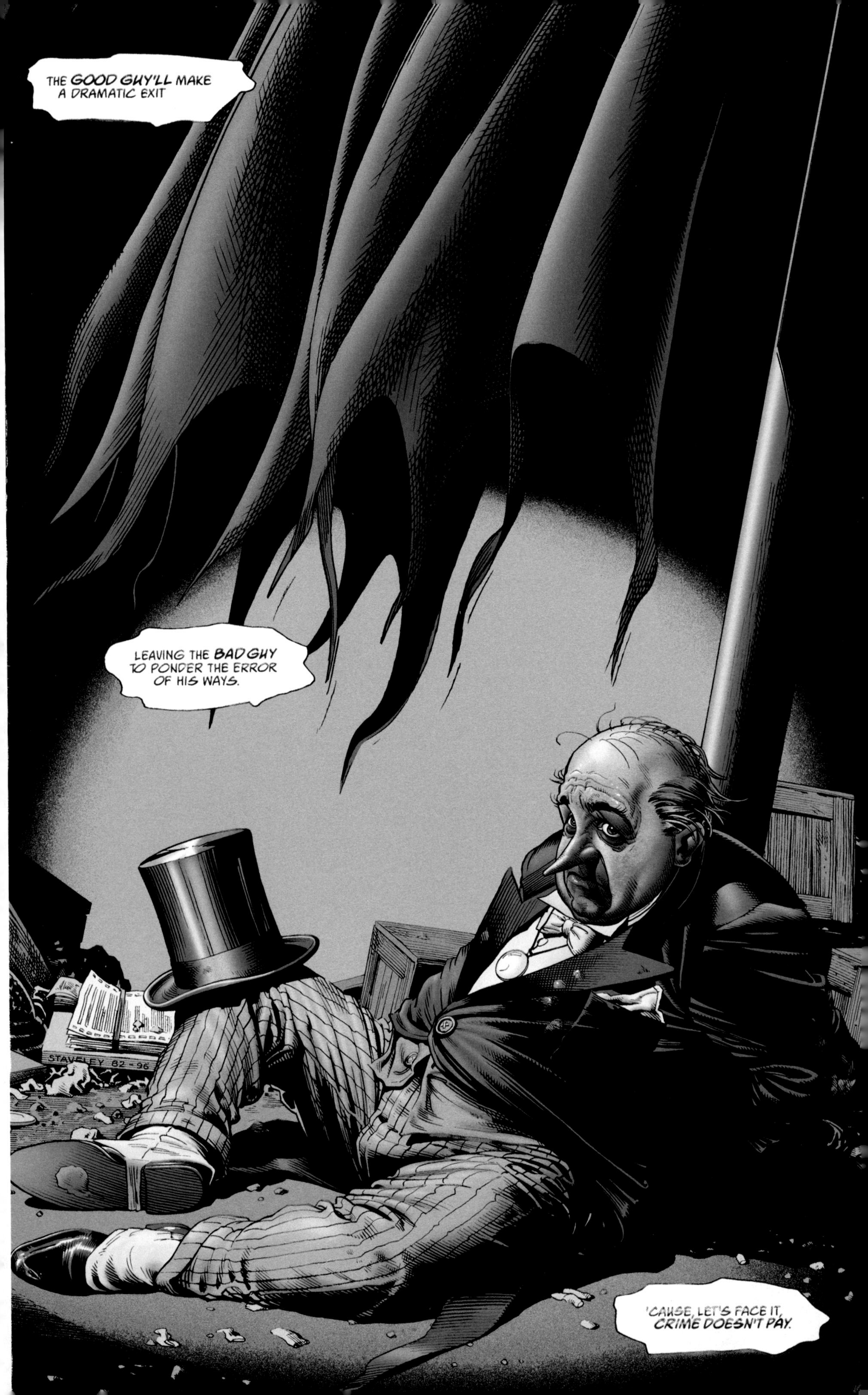
THE GOOD GUY'LL MAKE A DRAMATIC EXIT
LEAVING THE BAD GUY TO PONDER THE ERROR OF HIS WAYS.
STAVELEY 82-96
'CAUSE, LET'S FACE IT, CRIME DOESN'T PAY.

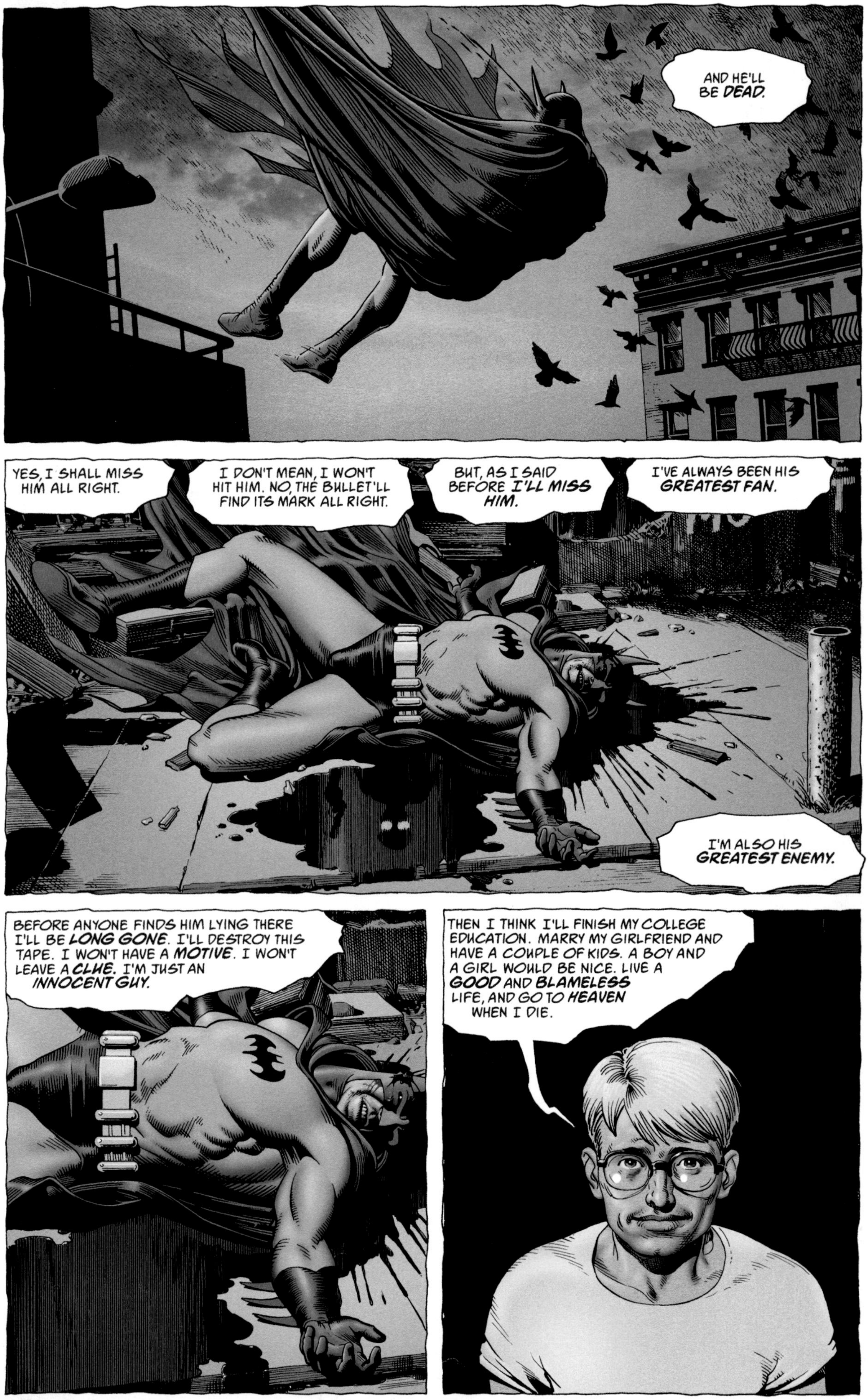
AND HE'LL BE DEAD.
YES, I SHALL MISS HIM ALL RIGHT.
I DON'T MEAN, I WON'T HIT HIM. NO, THE BULLET'LL FIND ITS MARK ALL RIGHT.
BUT, AS I SAID BEFORE I'LL MISS HIM.
I'VE ALWAYS BEEN HIS GREATEST FAN.
I'M ALSO HIS GREATEST ENEMY.
BEFORE ANYONE FINDS HIM LYING THERE I'LL BE LONG GONE. I'LL DESTROY THIS TAPE. I WON'T HAVE A MOTIVE. I WON'T LEAVE A CLUE. I'M JUST AN INNOCENT GUY.
THEN I THINK I'LL FINISH MY COLLEGE EDUCATION. MARRY MY GIRLFRIEND AND HAVE A COUPLE OF KIDS. A BOY AND A GIRL WOULD BE NICE. LIVE A GOOD AND BLAMELESS LIFE, AND GO TO HEAVEN WHEN I DIE.

From the files of Brian Bolland

Figures 1 and **2** are giving away a closely guarded professional secret. Yes, I did use photographic reference for the cover of THE KILLING JOKE! Since it's a mirror image of me in the photo you'll notice that it's actually the thumb of my left hand that's pressing the button to take the picture. The resulting sketch is probably the most thorough cover rough I've ever drawn and the only one in color. I must have been very keen to push the idea.

The evil dwarves (**figure 3**) were written into the script by Alan and given the names of three characters owned by another major company — so they can't be repeated here. I always wanted to apologize to any persons of diminutive stature who

As with the artwork, all the small "prelim" pages are now in the hands of collectors, and **figure 4** is the only one we could track down. I had more success with the *Innocent Guy* prelims. I have copies of some of them here (**figures 5,9,10**). This, incidentally, was the form in which I originally wrote the story and presented it to my editor, Mark Chiarello.

Figure 6 was drawn in Paris (with a series of markers that were running low on ink, by the looks of things) and Italian artist Tanino Liberatore produced a painted version of it for the French edition of THE KILLING JOKE. **Figures 7** and **8** are sketches of the Joker in his various guises.

ALAN MOORE

Alan Moore is perhaps the most acclaimed writer in the graphic story medium, having garnered countless awards for such works as WATCHMEN, V FOR VENDETTA, *From Hell*, *Miracleman* and SWAMP THING. He is also the mastermind behind the America's Best Comics line, through which he has created (along with many talented illustrators) THE LEAGUE OF EXTRAORDINARY GENTLEMEN, PROMETHEA, TOM STRONG, TOMORROW STORIES and TOP TEN. As one of the medium's most important innovators since the early 1980s, Moore has influenced an entire generation of comics creators, and his work continues to inspire an ever-growing audience. Moore resides in central England.

BRIAN BOLLAND

After making his professional debut in 1975, Brian Bolland perfected his clean-line style and meticulous attention to detail on a series of popular strips for the British comics magazine *2000 AD*, most notably its signature feature *Judge Dredd*. He went on to illustrate the 12-issue maxiseries *CAMELOT 3000* and BATMAN: THE KILLING JOKE for DC before shifting his focus to work almost exclusively on cover illustrations. Since then, he has earned a reputation as one of the best cover artists in the industry, and his elegantly composed and beautifully rendered pieces have graced a host of titles, including ANIMAL MAN, BATMAN, THE FLASH, THE INVISIBLES, WONDER WOMAN and many more.